Culture Wise
SPAIN

The Essential Guide to Culture, Customs & Business Etiquette

by

Joanna Styles

SURVIVAL BOOKS • LONDON • ENGLAND

First published 2007

Copyright © Survival Books 2007
Cover photograph © Elena Grogorova
Maps and cartoons © Jim Watson
Other photographs – see page 222

Survival Books Limited
26 York Street, London W1U 6PZ, United Kingdom
☎ +44 (0)20-7788 7644, 🖷 +44 (0)870-762 3212
✉ info@survivalbooks.net
💻 www.survivalbooks.net

British Library Cataloguing in Publication Data.
A CIP record for this book is available
from the British Library.
ISBN 10: 1-905303-19-X
ISBN 13: 978-1-905303-19-9

Printed and bound in India by Ajanta Offset

ACKNOWLEDGEMENTS

Many thanks to the members of my husband's family and the many Spanish friends who helped out with the finer points of Spanish etiquette. I would also like to thank Joe Laredo for the editing, Lilac Johnston for proof-reading, Di Tolland for the DTP, and Jim Watson for the book and cover design, maps and cartoons. Finally, a special thank you to all the photographers - the unsung heroes – who provided the superb photos, without which this book would be dull indeed.

THE AUTHOR

Joanna Styles (www.joannastyles.com) was born in London, but has lived and worked for many years on the Costa del Sol, Spain. She is a freelance writer and the author of several other books about Spain, including, *The Best Places to Buy a Home in Spain*, *Costa del Sol Lifeline, Earning Money From Your Spanish Home* and *Retiring in Spain,* all published by Survival Books. She also regularly updates many other Survival Books' publications. Joanna is married with two daughters.

'If you need to find out how France works then this book is indispensable. Native French people probably have a less thorough understanding of how their country functions.'

Living France

'It's everything you always wanted to ask but didn't for fear of the contemptuous put down. The best English-language guide. Its pages are stuffed with practical information on everyday subjects and are designed to compliment the traditional guidebook.'

Swiss News

'Rarely has a 'survival guide' contained such useful advice. This book dispels doubts for first-time travellers, yet is also useful for seasoned globetrotters. In a word, if you're planning to move to the US or go there for a long-term stay, then buy this book both for general reading and as a ready-reference.'

American Citizens Abroad

'Let's say it at once. David Hampshire's Living and Working in France is the best handbook ever produced for visitors and foreign residents in this country; indeed, my discussion with locals showed that it has much to teach even those born and bred in l'Hexagone. It is Hampshire's meticulous detail which lifts his work way beyond the range of other books with similar titles. Often you think of a supplementary question and search for the answer in vain. With Hampshire this is rarely the case. He writes with great clarity (and gives French equivalents of all key terms), a touch of humour and a ready eye for the odd (and often illuminating) fact. This book is absolutely indispensable.'

The Riviera Reporter

'A must for all future expats. I invested in several books but this is the only one you need. Every issue and concern is covered, every daft question you have but are frightened to ask is answered honestly without pulling any punches. Highly recommended.'

Reader

'In answer to the desert island question about the one how-to book on France, this book would be it.'

The Recorder

'The ultimate reference book. Every subject imaginable is exhaustively explained in simple terms. An excellent introduction to fully enjoy all that this fine country has to offer and save time and money in the process.'

American Club of Zurich

SAID ABOUT SURVIVAL BOOKS

'The amount of information covered is not short of incredible. I thought I knew enough about my birth country. This book has proved me wrong. Don't go to France without it. Big mistake if you do. Absolutely priceless!'

Reader

'When you buy a model plane for your child, a video recorder, or some new computer gizmo, you get with it a leaflet or booklet pleading 'Read Me First', or bearing large friendly letters or bold type saying 'IMPORTANT – follow the instructions carefully'. This book should be similarly supplied to all those entering France with anything more durable than a 5-day return ticket. It is worth reading even if you are just visiting briefly, or if you have lived here for years and feel totally knowledgeable and secure. But if you need to find out how France works then it is indispensable. Native French people probably have a less thorough understanding of how their country functions. Where it is most essential, the book is most up to the minute.

Living France

A comprehensive guide to all things French, written in a highly readable and amusing style, for anyone planning to live, work or retire in France.

The Times

Covers every conceivable question that might be asked concerning everyday life . I know of no other book that could take the place of this one.

France in Print

A concise, thorough account of the Do's and DONT's for a foreigner in Switzerland. Crammed with useful information and lightened with humorous quips which make the facts more readable.

American Citizens Abroad

'I found this a wonderful book crammed with facts and figures, with a straightforward approach to the problems and pitfalls you are likely to encounter. The whole laced with humour and a thorough understanding of what's involved. Gets my vote!'

Reader

'A vital tool in the war against real estate sharks; don't even think of buying without reading this book first!'

Everything Spain

'We would like to congratulate you on this work: it is really super! We hand it out to our expatriates and they read it with great interest and pleasure.'

ICI (Switzerland) AG

CONTENTS

INTRODUCTION

If you're planning a trip to Spain or just want to learn more about the country, you'll find the information contained in *Culture Wise Spain* invaluable. Whether you're travelling on business or pleasure, visiting for a few days or planning to stay forever, Culture Wise guides enable you to quickly find your feet by removing the anxiety factor when dealing with a foreign culture.

Culture Wise Spain is essential reading for anyone planning to visit Spain, including, tourists, business people, migrants, retirees and holiday homeowners. It's designed to help newcomers avoid cultural and social gaffes; make friends and influence people; improve communications (both verbal and non-verbal); and enhance their understanding of Spain and the Spanish people. It explains what to expect, how to behave in most situations, and how to get along with the locals and feel at home – rather than feeling like a fish out of water.

Spain is a hugely popular holiday destination and the leading European country for second homes and retirement. On the face of it, it seems an 'easy' option, with millions of visitors from all corners of the globe and well-established expatriate communities. But, don't be deceived: adjusting to a different environment and culture in any foreign country can be a traumatic and stressful experience, and Spain is no exception. You need to adapt to new customs and traditions, and discover the Spanish way of doing things; whether it's eating dinner at nearly midnight, adjusting to Spain's frenetic driving conditions (and driving on the right-hand side of the road) or dealing with the country's oppressive bureaucracy.

Spain is a nation with a deep-rooted culture – perhaps more so than any other Western European country – where traditions and the traditional way of life remain strong. It isn't simply a sunny spot where you can eat out cheaply but an extremely diverse country populated by an even more diverse people (or peoples), whose character and culture are deeply embedded in everyday life. Above all, it's a country with an irrepressible lifestyle, a land of (almost) perpetual sunshine, where the people live life to the fullest.

A period spent in Spain is a wonderful way to enrich your life, broaden your horizons, and hopefully expand your circle of friends. I trust this book will help you avoid the pitfalls of visiting or living in Spain and smooth your way to a happy and rewarding stay.

¡Suerte!

Joanna Styles
July 2007

Park Güell, Barcelona

1.
A CHANGE OF CULTURE

With almost daily advances in technology, ever-cheaper flights and knowledge about almost anywhere in the world at our fingertips, travelling, living, working and retiring abroad have never been more accessible, and current migration patterns suggest that it has never been more popular. But, although globalisation means the world has 'shrunk', every country is still a world of its own with a unique culture.

Some people find it impossible to adapt to a new life in a different culture – for reasons which are many and varied. According to statistics, partner dissatisfaction is the most common cause, as non-working spouses frequently find themselves without a role in the new country and sometimes with little to do other than think about what they would be doing if they were at home. Family concerns – which may include the children's education and worries about loved ones at home – can also deeply affect those living abroad.

Many factors contribute to how well you adapt to a new culture – for example your personality, education, foreign language skills, mental health, maturity, socio-economic situation, travel experience, and family and social support systems. How you handle the stress of change and bring balance and meaning to your life is the principal indicator of how well you'll adjust to a different country, culture and business environment.

> 'There are no foreign lands. It is the traveller only who is foreign.'
>
> Robert Louis Stevenson (Scottish writer)

SPAIN IS DIFFERENT

Many people underestimate the cultural isolation that can be experienced in a foreign country, particularly one with a different language. Even in a country where you speak the language fluently you'll find that many aspects of the culture are surprisingly foreign (despite the cosy familiarity engendered by cinema, television and books).

Spain is popularly perceived by many foreigners – particularly the British – as an easy expatriate option because of its well established foreign communities the length and breadth of its Mediterranean coast.

However, despite the widespread availability of all-day English breakfasts and *The Daily Mail*, it's difficult to avoid the real Spain and Spanish culture. Moving to a *Costa* might be simpler than moving to, say, Madrid to begin with, but sooner or later culture shock sets in. When you move to Spain you'll need to adapt to a totally new environment and new challenges, which may include a new job, a new home and a new physical environment, which can be overwhelming – and all this before you even encounter the local culture. Those who move to a new job in Spain may encounter a (very) steep learning curve. The chances are that you've left a job in your home country where you held a senior position, were extremely competent and knew all your colleagues. In Spain, you may be virtually a trainee (especially if your Spanish isn't fluent) and not know any of your colleagues.

The sensation that you're starting from scratch can be demoralising.

> Spain has many extremes of climate and weather, and you mustn't underestimate the effects that these can have on you. Extreme conditions of heat and cold can lead to a lack of energy, poor sleep and dehydration. In the summer in many parts of Spain, air-conditioning is common and if you aren't used to this it can be draining.

Even if you move to a part of Spain with a well established expatriate community, items that you're used to and took for granted in your home country may not be available, e.g. certain kinds of food, opportunities to engage in your favourite hobby or sport, books and television programmes in your language. The lack of 'home comforts' can wear you down. You'll also have to contend with the lack of a local support network. At home you had a circle of friends, acquaintances, colleagues and possibly relatives you could rely on for help and support. In Spain, there's no such network, which can leave you feeling lost.

The degree of isolation you feel usually depends on how long you plan to spend in Spain and what you'll be doing there. If you're simply going on a short holiday you may not even be aware of many of the cultural differences, although if you are, it will enhance your enjoyment and may save you a few embarrassing or confusing moments.

However, if you're planning a business trip or intend to spend an extended period in Spain, perhaps working, studying or even living there permanently, **it's essential to understand the culture, customs and etiquette at the earliest opportunity.**

CULTURE SHOCK

Culture shock is the term used to describe the psychological and physical state felt by people when arriving in a foreign country. It can even affect people moving to a new environment in their home country, where the culture, and in some cases language, may vary considerably by region or social class. Culture shock can be experienced when travelling, living, working or studying abroad, when in addition to adapting to new social rules and values, you may need to adjust to a different climate, food and dress. It manifests itself in a lack of direction and the feeling of not knowing what to do or how to do things, not knowing what's appropriate or inappropriate.

> 'When you travel, remember that a foreign country is not designed to make you comfortable. It is designed to make its own people comfortable.'

You literally feel like a fish out of water. Culture shock is precipitated by the anxiety that results from losing all familiar rules of behaviour and cues to social intercourse – the thousand and one clues to behaviour in everyday situations: when to shake hands and what to say when we meet people; how to buy goods and services; when and how much to tip; how to use a cash machine or the

telephone; when to accept and refuse invitations; and when to take statements seriously and when not to. These cues, which may be words, gestures or facial expressions, are acquired in the course of our life and are as much a part of our culture and customs as the language we speak and our beliefs. Our peace of mind and social efficiency depends on these cues, most of which are unconsciously recognised. The symptoms of culture shock are essentially psychological – although you can experience physical pain from culture shock – and are caused by the sense of alienation you feel when you're bombarded on a daily basis by cultural differences in an environment where there are few, if any, familiar references.

However, there are also physical symptoms including an increased incidence of minor illnesses (e.g. colds and headaches) and more serious psychosomatic illnesses brought on by depression. You shouldn't underestimate the consequences of culture shock, although the effects can be lessened if you accept the condition rather than deny it.

Stages of Culture Shock

Severe culture shock – often experienced when moving to a country with a different language – usually follows a number of stages. The names of these may vary, as may the symptoms and effects, but a typical progression is as follows:

1. The first stage is commonly known as the 'honeymoon' stage and usually lasts from a few days to a few weeks after arrival (although it can last longer, particularly if you're insulated from the usual pressures of life). This stage is essentially a positive (even euphoric) one, when a newcomer finds everything an exciting and interesting novelty. The feeling is similar to being on holiday or a short trip abroad, when you generally experience only the positive effects of culture shock (although this depends very much on where you're from and the country you're visiting – see box).

2. The second (rejection or distress) stage is usually completely opposite to the first and is essentially negative and a period of crisis, as the initial excitement and holiday feeling wears off and you start to cope with the real conditions of daily life – except of course that life is nothing like anything you've previously experienced. This can happen after only a few weeks and is characterised by a general feeling of disorientation, confusion and loneliness. Physical exhaustion brought on by a change of time zone, extremes of hot or cold, and the strain of having hundreds of settling-in tasks to accomplish is an important symptom of this stage. You may also experience regression, where you spend much of your time speaking your own language, watching television and reading newspapers

Every year, a dozen or so Japanese tourists have to be repatriated from the French capital after falling prey to what has become known as 'Paris Syndrome'. This is what some polite Japanese tourists suffer when they discover that Parisians can be rude or that the city doesn't meet their expectations. The experience can be so stressful that they suffer a nervous breakdown and need to be hospitalised or repatriated under medical supervision.

from your home country, eating food from home and socialising with expatriates who speak your language. You may also spend a lot of time complaining about the host country and its culture.

Your home environment suddenly assumes a tremendous importance and is irrationally glorified. All difficulties and problems are forgotten and only the good things back home are remembered.

> The transition between your old culture and customs and those of your new country is a difficult one and takes time to complete. During this process there can be strong feelings of dissatisfaction. The period of readjustment can last six months, although there are expatriates who adjust earlier and (although rare) those who never get over the 'flight' stage and are forced to return home.

3. The third stage is often known as the 'flight' stage (because of the overwhelming desire to escape) and is usually the one that lasts the longest and is the most difficult to cope with. During this period you may feel depressed and angry, as well as resentful towards the new country and its people.

You may experience difficulties such as not being understood and feelings of discontent, impatience, frustration, sadness and incompetence. These feelings are inevitable when you're trying to adapt to a new culture

that's very different from that of your home country, and they're exacerbated by the fact that you can see nothing positive or good about the new country and focus exclusively on the negative aspects, refusing to acknowledge any positive points. You may become hostile and develop an aggressive attitude towards the country.

Other people will sense this and in many cases either respond in a confrontational manner or try to avoid you. There may be problems with the language, your house, job or children's school, transportation ... even simple tasks like shopping may be fraught with problems, and the fact that the local people are largely indifferent to all these problems only makes matter worse. They try to help but they just don't understand your concerns, and you conclude that they must be insensitive and unsympathetic to you and your problems.

4. The fourth (recovery or autonomy) stage is where you

begin to integrate and adjust to the new culture and accept the customs of the country as simply another way of living. **The environment doesn't change – what changes is your attitude towards it.** You become more competent with the language and you also feel more comfortable with the customs of the host country and can move around without feeling anxiety. However, you still have problems with some of the social cues and you won't understand everything people say (particularly colloquialisms and idioms). Nevertheless, you have largely adjusted to the new culture and start to feel more at home and familiar with the country and your place in it, and begin to realise that it has its good as well as bad points.

> 'Travellers never think that THEY are the foreigners.'
>
> Mason Cooley (American aphorist)

5. The fifth stage is termed 'reverse culture shock' and occurs when you return to your home country. You may find that many things have changed (you will also have changed) and that you feel like a foreigner in your own country. If you've been away for a long time and have become comfortable with the habits and customs of a new lifestyle, you may find that you no longer feel at ease in your homeland. Reverse culture shock can be difficult to deal with and some people find it impossible to re-adapt to their home country after living abroad for a number of years.

The above stages occur at different times depending on the individual and his circumstances, and everyone has his own way of reacting to them, with the result that some stages last longer and are more difficult to cope with than others, while others are shorter and easier to overcome.

Reducing the Effects

Experts agree that almost everyone suffers from culture shock and there's no escaping the phenomenon; however, its negative effects can be reduced considerably and there are certain things you can do even before leaving home:

Toledo

● **Positive attitude** – The key to reducing the negative effects of culture shock is a positive attitude towards Spain (whether you're visiting or planning to live there) – if you don't look forward to a holiday or relocation, you should question why you're doing it. There's no greater guarantee for unhappiness in a foreign environment than taking your prejudices with you. It's important when trying to adapt to a new culture to be sensitive to the locals' feelings and try to put yourself in their shoes wherever possible, which will help you understand why they react as they do. Bear in mind that they have a strong, in-bred cultural code, just as you do, and react in certain ways because they're culturally 'trained' to do so. If you find yourself frustrated by an aspect of the local culture or behaviour,

the chances are that they will be equally puzzled by yours.

● **Research** – Discover as much as possible about Spain before you go, so that your arrival and settling-in period doesn't spring as many surprises as it might otherwise. Reading up on Spain and its culture before you leave home will help you familiarise yourself with the local customs and language, and make the country and its people seem less strange on arrival. You'll be aware of many of the differences in Spain and be better prepared to deal with them. This will help you avoid being upset by real or imaginary cultural slights and also reduce the chance of your offending the locals by cultural misunderstandings.

> Culture shock is an unavoidable part of travelling, living and working abroad, but if you're aware of it and take steps to lessen its effects before you go and while you're abroad, the period of adjustment will be shortened and its negative and depressing consequences reduced.

Being prepared for a certain amount of disorientation and confusion (or worse) makes it easier to cope with it. There are literally hundreds of publications about Spain as well as dozens of websites for expatriates (see Appendices B and C). Many sites provide access to expatriates already living in Spain who can answer questions and provide useful advice. There are also 'notice boards' on many websites where you can post messages or questions.

● **Visit Spain first** – If you're planning to live or work in Spain for a number of years or even permanently, it's important to visit the country to see whether you think you would enjoy living there and be able to cope with the culture before making the leap. Before you go, try to find someone who has visited Spain and talk to him about it. Some companies organise briefings for families before departure. Rent a property before buying a home and don't burn your bridges until you're certain that you've made the right decision.

Mojacar, Almeria

● **Learn Spanish** – Along with adopting a positive attitude, overcoming the language barrier will probably be the most decisive factor in combating culture shock and enjoying your time in Spain. The ability to speak Spanish (or the local language – see **Chapter 5**) isn't just a practical and useful tool (that will allow you to buy what you need, find your way around, etc.) but the key to understanding Spain and its culture. If you can speak the language, even at a low level, your scope for making friends is immediately widened beyond the limited expatriate circle.

Obviously not everyone is a linguist and learning a language can take time and requires motivation. However, with sufficient perseverance virtually anyone can learn enough of another language to participate in the local culture. Certainly the effort will pay off and expatriates who manage to overcome the language barrier find their experience in Spain much richer and more rewarding than those who don't. If you make an effort at communicating with the local people in their own language, you'll also find them far more receptive to you and your needs.

● **Be proactive** – Make an effort to get involved in your new culture and go out of your way to make friends. Join in the activities of the local people, which could be a carnival, a religious festival or

> 'And that's the wonderful thing about family travel: it provides you with experiences that will remain locked forever in the scar tissue of your mind.'
>
> Dave Barry (American writer & humorist)

a social activity. There are often plenty of local clubs where you can engage in sport or keep fit, draw and paint, learn to cook local dishes, taste wine, etc. Not only will this fill some of your spare time, giving you less time to miss home, but you'll also meet people and make new friends. If you feel you cannot join a local club, perhaps because the language barrier is too great, then you can always participate in activities for expatriates, of which there are many in the most popular destinations. Look upon a period spent abroad as an opportunity to redefine your life objectives and acquire new perspectives. Culture shock can help you develop a better understanding of yourself and stimulate your creativity.

- **Talk to other expatriates** – Although they may deny it, they've all been through exactly what you're experiencing and faced the same feelings of disorientation. Even if they cannot provide you with advice, it helps to know that you aren't alone and that it gets better over time. However, don't make the mistake of mixing only with expatriates as this will alienate you from the local culture and make it much harder to integrate. Don't rely on social contact with your compatriots to carry you through, because it won't.

> 'The whole object of travel is not to set foot on foreign land; it is at last to set foot on one's own country as a foreign land. '
>
> G. K. Chesterton (English writer)

- **Keep in touch with home** – Keeping in touch with your family and friends at home and around the world by telephone, email and letters will help reduce and overcome the effects of culture shock.

- **Be happy** – Don't rely others to make you happy; otherwise you won't find true and lasting happiness. There are things in life which you can change and if you need them to change you must do it yourself. Every day we are surrounded by things over which we have little or no control and to wail about them only makes us unhappier. So be your own best friend and nurture your own capacity for happiness.

Avila

FAMILIES IN SPAIN

Family life may be completely different in Spain and relationships can become strained under the stress of adapting to culture shock. Your family may find itself in a completely new and possibly alien environment, your new home may scarcely resemble your previous one (it may be much more luxurious or significantly smaller) and the climate may be dramatically different from that of your home country. If possible, you should prepare yourself for as many aspects of the new situation as you can and explain to your children the differences they're likely to encounter, while at the same time dispelling their fears.

In a situation where one spouse is working (usually the husband) and the other not, it's usually the latter (and any children) who's more affected by culture shock. The husband has his work to occupy him and his activities may not differ much from what he'd been accustomed to at home. On the other hand, the wife has to operate in a totally new environment, which differs considerably from what she's used to. She will find herself alone more often, as there will be no close relatives or friends on hand.

However, if you're aware that this situation may arise, you can take action to reduce its effects. Working spouses should pay special attention to the needs and feelings of their non-working partners and children, as the success of a family relocation depends on the ability of the wife and children to adapt to the new culture.

Good communication between family members is vital and you should make time to discuss your experiences and feelings, both as a couple and as a family. Questions should always be raised and, if

> 'If you reject the food, ignore the customs, fear the religion and avoid the people, you might better stay at home.'
>
> James A. Michener (American writer)

possible, answered, particularly when asked by children. However difficult your situation may appear at the beginning, it will help to bear in mind that it's by no means unique and that most expatriate families experience exactly the same problems, and manage to triumph over them and thoroughly enjoy their stay abroad.

A NEW LIFE

Although you may find some of the information in this chapter a bit daunting, don't be discouraged by the foregoing catalogue of depression and despair; the negative aspects of travelling and living abroad have been highlighted only in order to help you prepare and adjust to a new life. The vast majority of people who travel and live abroad naturally experience occasional feelings of discomfort and disorientation, **but most never suffer the most debilitating effects of culture shock.**

As with settling in and making friends anywhere, even in your home country, the most important thing is to be considerate, kind, open, humble and genuine – qualities that are valued the world over. Selfishness, brashness and arrogance will get you nowhere in Spain or any other country. Treat Spain and its people with respect and they will do likewise.

The majority of people living in a foreign land would agree that, all things considered, they love living there – and are in no hurry to return home. A period spent abroad is a wonderful way to enrich your life, broaden your horizons, make new friends and maybe even please your bank manager. We trust that this book will help you to avoid some of the pitfalls of life abroad and smooth your way to a happy and rewarding future in your new home.

> 'Twenty years from now you will be more disappointed by the things you didn't do than by the ones you did do. So throw off the bowlines. Sail away from the safe harbour. Catch the trade winds in your sails. Explore. Dream. Discover.'
>
> Mark Twain (American author)

2.

WHO ARE THE SPANISH?

For years, Europe's second-largest country has tempted foreigners to its shores, and nowadays Spain is more popular than ever: it tops the European retirement location charts and, with over 55m visitors annually, it's the world's second-most popular tourist destination after France. It's also a popular relocation spot, not only for those from less-developed countries looking for better opportunities in the buoyant job market, but also for thousands of European Union (EU) citizens attracted by the unique combination of sunshine, low cost of living and relaxed lifestyle.

But Spain isn't just a sunny spot where you can eat out cheaply: it's an extremely diverse country populated by an even more diverse people, whose character and culture are deeply embedded in everyday life.

The regional variety found in Spain is perhaps unique in Europe and few countries can rival it for contrast. Its contrasts mostly co-exist peacefully, but every so often they clash – Spain has a chequered history and is the EU country with the most recent civil war and dictatorship. However, although they don't agree on many things, the Spaniards are unanimous that 'Spain is different' (not for nothing was this the Tourist Board's slogan during the '80s).

> America is named after Amerigo Vespucci, a member of Columbus's crew and the first person to realise that they had discovered a new continent.

To help explain this diversity and who the Spanish are, this chapter provides information on Spain's history and the Spaniards' character. A list of Spanish cultural icons can also be found here.

TIMELINE

Like many other European countries, Spain has a rich and chequered history. The main events are as follows:

First Arrivals

400,000 years ago – First inhabitants are cave dwellers and their remains provide some of the world's most important clues to prehistoric man.

5,000BC – Celts inhabit much of the north of the peninsula; recent research suggests that they originated in Galicia, from where they migrated to Ireland, Britain and France.

800BC – The Phoenicians, who establish many maritime settlements, including Cadiz, Europe's oldest city.

600BC – The Greeks, who go no further than the north-east of the peninsula

200BC – The Romans, who stay for

several centuries and leave a lasting architectural legacy.

400AD – The Visigoths.

The Moors

From 711AD, the Moors, arriving from Africa and Arabia, take over most of the peninsula (with the exception of the north-west) and stay for almost 800 years. Their civilisation, known as Al-Andalus, is highly cultured and learned, and with its court patronage of mathematics, astronomy, engineering and medicine becomes one of the world's most sophisticated societies.

The Moors are responsible for installing vast systems of irrigation on agricultural land (many of which survive today) and several architectural gems, including the Alhambra (Spain's most visited tourist attraction), the Mosque and Medina Zahara settlement in Córdoba, and the Giralda tower adjoining Seville's cathedral.

Perhaps the Moors' most remarkable achievement is the peaceful co-existence between Christians, Jews and Muslims.

The Birth of Modern Spain

1492 – The 'reconquest' of Spain culminates when Ferdinand and Isabel, the Catholic Monarchs, expel the last of the Moors and take Granada, giving rise to the nation of Spain as we know it today. 1492 is also the year Christopher Columbus initiates Spain's huge empire when he becomes the first European to cross the Atlantic.

1517 – Spain claims much of Central and South America (except Brazil), the peninsula of Florida, part of California and the Philippines. Under Charles V and later Philip II, Spain's empire also includes Sicily, Sardinia, the kingdom of Naples, Milan and Flanders. The Spanish empire thus becomes the most important in the world.

Demographics

Population: 44.1m.

Population density: 80 inhabitants per km^2 (200 per square mile). Barcelona and Madrid have a density of 600 inhabitants per km^2 (1,600 per square mile).

Largest cities: Madrid (3.2m), Barcelona (1.6m), Valencia (796,600), Seville (704,000) and Zaragoza (647,300).

Foreign population: 3.75m (8.5 per cent).

Largest expatriate groups: Moroccan, Ecuadorian and Romanian.

State religion: Spain is officially a secular state.

Riches from the New World bring huge prosperity to Spain, although few Spaniards benefit other than those at Court or in the upper echelons of society.

> 'From the beginning of history to the sixteenth century, the Spaniards gradually climbed towards the pinnacle of their success (...) steadily accumulating wealth, culture, prestige and unity. From the 16th century until our times, they've been almost constantly slithering downhill (...). Spanish history does not form a happy pattern, but at least it looks symmetrical.'
>
> Jan Morris, *Spain*

The Golden Age

The 17th century is known as the Golden Age and produces some of Spain's greatest literature and art – *Don Quixote* (the world's first novel) by Cervantes, Lope de Vega's plays and Velázquez's paintings.

1665 – Territory is lost within Europe and Spain's decline commences.

1793-95 – Spain loses war against France, leading to an alliance with Napoleon.

1797-1805 – War against Great Britain culminating in the Battle of Trafalgar, which Spain loses.

1808-14 – War of Independence, against the French presence in Spain. French troops are finally expelled.

1812 – Spain's first liberal Constitution is approved in Cádiz but quickly overturned.

1819-24 – All Spain's colonies gain independence except Cuba, Puerto Rico and the Philippines.

1873-74 – First Republic, but it's overturned by a military coup and the monarchy restored.

1898 – The loss of the remaining colonies signifies the end of Spain's empire and leads to national depression. Spain is finally forced to look inwards and solve its acute problems of poverty and inequality.

20th Century

Spain is deeply divided into a small, rich land-owning class and a majority of poverty-stricken workers and landless peasants. The Catholic Church exercises enormous power and the strong military sees itself as the guardian of traditional Spain. The regions of Catalonia and the Basque Country continue their bid for autonomy.

Against an international backdrop of revolutionary uprisings, the emergence of Fascism and Communism and the instability of Europe, Spain's social and political situation from 1898 to 1939 is one of continual upheaval and civil strife.

1923 – Military coup led by Primo de Rivera, who establishes a military dictatorship with the support of King Alfonso XIII.

1931 – Elections result in an overwhelming victory for the Republican parties. Alfonso XIII is forced to abdicate, a centuries-old tradition of monarchy ends and a Republic is declared – all in a single day.

1931-36 – Spain's Second Republic, five years of ambitious reforms and continued social strife and political polarisation.

1936-39 – Civil War in which more than 350,000 Spaniards are killed.

> It usually isn't wise to mention either the Civil War or Franco in conversation, as feelings run high on both topics.

The war ends with General Franco's Nationalist victory. Republicans are imprisoned, exiled or executed.

The Spanish Civil War is one of the world's most written-about events – there are some 1,600 novels alone. Hemingway's *For Whom the Bell Tolls* is one of the most famous.

1939-50 – The rest of the world shuns Franco's regime and Spain lives in poverty under a system of autarchy.

1950-70 – The US implements its 'Marshall Plan' in Spain in exchange for military bases and this, together with emerging industry and tourism, leads to economic growth and prosperity. Spain is admitted to the UN in 1955.

1975 – Franco dies, having named King Juan Carlos as head of state. Instead of continuing the dictatorship, the king sets the wheels of democracy in motion.

1977 – First democratic elections since 1936 won by the UCD, a centre-right party.

1978 – Spaniards approve the Constitution and Spain becomes a parliamentary monarchy.

1981 – A military coup takes the congress hostage, but the king's support of democracy and his order that the army, which is under his command, stay loyal to the constitution means that it fails.

1982 – Overwhelming victory for the PSOE (Socialist party) under Felipe González.

1986 – Spain joins the EU.

1992 – Spain's 'Golden Year' with the Olympic Games in Barcelona and Expo 92 in Seville celebrating the 500th anniversary of Columbus's discovery of America.

1996 – The right-wing PP (Partido Popular) led by José María Aznar wins the election, but without a majority is forced to ally with the Basque and Catalan parties in parliament.

21st Century

2000 – The PP wins a second term, this time with an overall majority.
2002 – The euro replaces the peseta as Spain's official currency.
2004 – 191 people are killed in four train explosions in Madrid, three days before general elections. Evidence points to a cell belonging to Al-Qaida as responsible for the bombing, but Aznar's government insists on blaming ETA. The PSOE wins the general election, but not with a majority.
2006 – ETA, the Basque separatist and terrorist group formed in 1959 and responsible for over 300 killings, declares an indefinite ceasefire. Expectations of an end to ETA violence were dashed when ETA exploded a massive bomb in a car park at Madrid's Barajas airport, killing two people.

THE PEOPLE

Spain's widespread territory and varied geography, coupled with a history of invasion, emigration and immigration have resulted in great diversity among its population and it's impossible to list the characteristics of a 'typical Spaniard'. A recent nationwide survey asked Spaniards to define themselves, and the majority claimed to be kind, 'reasonably responsible', hardworking (without being workaholics), honest and moderately progressive. According to the same survey, Spaniards consider themselves to have no salient good points, but no outstandingly bad ones either.

> A survey carried out in 1988 when democracy was young asked the following question: 'Do you consider yourself qualified to be a good president of Spain?' An amazing 13.4 per cent of Spaniards said yes.

Apart from the differences in character between the inhabitants of different regions, such as Andalusia, the Basque Country, Catalonia, Galicia and Madrid – not to mention the Balearic and Canary Islands – there are the influences of a potpourri of foreigners from all over the globe to take into account. Even in appearance, fewer and fewer Spaniards match the popular image of short, swarthy and dark, and the indigenous population includes blondes, brunettes and redheads; and Spanish teenagers are now as tall as their counterparts throughout Europe.

But in spite of their many differences, most Spaniards share some characteristics – principally the following:

Individualism

The Spaniard is essentially individualistic and the main (often, the only) player in his life. From this stems the strong anarchic streak in the Spanish character, the Spaniard's penchant for doing whatever he (or she) likes – interpreting regulations on a whim, parking anywhere, not paying taxes, making noise at all hours …

Generosity

The Spanish are generous almost without limits and willing to share what they have (however little) with others. This generosity means that newcomers to Spain are welcomed almost everywhere and invited to join in. Spaniards are also generous with their time and help – most go out of their way to lend a hand when it's needed.

> 'In every Spaniard's passport are the following invisible words: "This Spaniard is authorised to do whatever he wants.'
>
> Angel Ganivet (1865-98), essayist and philosopher

Impetuousness

An essential part of Spanish culture is the almost complete absence of fear of death or perhaps a blind faith in immortality. This trait leads to impetuous and often reckless action – this is after all one of the few countries in the world where standing defenceless in front of a massive charging bull is regarded as accepted behaviour. For this reason Spaniards often drive recklessly, frequently don't wear seatbelts or helmets and have one of the EU's highest work accident rates – un-harnessed workmen painting the façade of high-rise buildings and helmet-less crane operators are a common sight.

This tendency to 'live on the edge' may also account for the reluctance of most Spaniards to plan anything in detail, preferring to leave everything to chance – or rather crossing their fingers and **hoping** it will turn out all right.

As a result, many aspects of daily life are highly disorganised and the only predictable thing about them is their unpredictability. If something is planned, the plans are invariably changed or abandoned at the last moment, as one of the hallmarks of Spanish life is spontaneity.

Joie de Vivre

For sheer vitality and exuberance the Spanish have few equals, and whatever Spain can be accused of, it's never dull or boring. Few other countries offer such a wealth of intoxicating experiences for the mind, body and spirit (and not all out of a bottle). The Spaniards relish the present and live life to its very fullest whenever possible – and this irrepressible *joie de vivre* (surprisingly, there's no equivalent Spanish term) is highly contagious. Spanish parties are among the world's loudest, wildest and most colourful, and (best of all) anyone can join in.

> 'We Spaniards know a sickness of the heart that only gold can cure.'
>
> Hernán Cortés (16th century explorer)

In Spain, work fits around social and family life, not vice versa – the Spaniards may be one of the few nations in Europe that have this right – and the foundation of Spanish society is the family and community, not a job and money. Perhaps not surprisingly, the Spanish have one of the highest life expectancies in the world and one of the lowest incidences of stress-related disease.

Mañana Syndrome

The Spanish are dismissive of time constraints and have no sense of urgency and even less respect for appointments, dates, opening hours and timetables. This is the infamous *mañana* syndrome, where everything is possible 'tomorrow' – which can mean later, much later, some time, the day after tomorrow, next week, next month, next year or never – but never, ever tomorrow (the Spaniard's motto is 'Never do today what you can put off until *mañana*'). When a workman says he will come at 11 o'clock, don't forget to ask which day, month and year he has in mind.

Workmen (especially plumbers) don't usually keep appointments and, if they do deign to make an appearance on the appointed day, they're invariably late.

Pride

For most observers of the Spanish character including Spaniards themselves, pride is an intrinsic part of the Spanish psyche and one that explains much of their behaviour. The chapter on pride in essayist Fernando Díaz-Plaja's book *Seven Deadly Sins* is by far the longest.

Because of their pride, most Spaniards always present an immaculate exterior to the outside world and regard family and social occasions as a means of showing others how well-to-do they are. In many homes the main (and largest) room is richly decorated and laid out like a museum, with the best family furniture and fittings on display. The family rarely enters this room (let alone uses it), which is purely for receiving visitors.

Even those with modest incomes spend small fortunes on clothes and cars and will readily treat others to a drink or meal in an attempt to present a favourable impression. Spaniards are preoccupied by what others may think of them – '*el qué dirán*' (what others will say) – and there's a strong sense that when you're out, you need to be on your best behaviour. A consequence of this is the Spaniards' dislike of being laughed at or teased and most find it difficult to laugh at themselves. The fear of ridicule runs deep in their

> The Spanish language is full of derogatory sayings about the inhabitants of other regions, e.g.
> '**Hijos de Madrid: uno bueno entre mil.**' (People from Madrid: one good one in a thousand)
> '**Antes marrano que murciano.**' (Better to be a pig than from Murcia)
> '**Granadino, ladrón fino.**' (A man from Granada, a classy thief)
> '**Buena es Cuenca para ciegos.**' (Cuenca's only good for the blind)

veins and most go to great lengths to avoid anything that might expose them to appearing silly in front of others.

Self-importance leads many Spaniards to believe that manual work is below them – few students 'stoop' to casual employment as a means of supplementing their studies – whereas having a job where you wear a suit is seen as highly desirable, indicating that you've done well in life.

Pride also means that Spaniards defend their country and their way of doing things to the last – it's very difficult to get a Spaniard to 'see' that there are alternative methods and impossible to make him understand that these could perhaps be better. It therefore follows that according to the Spaniards, Spanish wine, food and customs are almost always superior to any others.

Regionalism

Although few topics unite Spaniards more than the superiority of Spain over other countries, this national pride disappears as soon as a Spaniard is in the company of his compatriots. For any Spaniard, his region, province, town or village is far superior to any other in Spain and he will defend it against all odds. Spain's succession of invaders found pockets of resistance every step of the way – the Romans took nine years to invade France, but nearly 200 to conquer Spain.

Spaniards aren't really from Spain but from their home town and therefore see themselves as quite different from other Spaniards. However, instead of using this as a celebration of the richness of their country's culture, they use it as a bone of contention and are frequently disparaging about their compatriots from other regions. Nobody understands the Basques and their tongue-twister of a language, the Galicians are derided as being more Portuguese than Spanish, and the Andalusians are scorned as backward peasants. However, the most intense antagonism is between the cities of Madrid and Barcelona, whose inhabitants argue about everything, including the economy, sport, history, politics, culture and language. Catalans claim that *Madrileños* are half African, to which the latter reply that it's better than being half French ...

HUMOUR

Humour is one of the subtlest forms of cultural expression and, as every expat knows, there are few more

uncomfortable situations than being the only one not roaring with laughter at a joke and few more alienating than not understanding a pun or being unable to join in witty repartee. However, not 'getting' the humour is part and parcel of culture shock and something you'll have to learn to accept until your language skills have advanced sufficiently for you to appreciate its subtleties.

The good news about Spanish humour is that it isn't too difficult to understand – subtle irony and sarcasm don't play a big part, although the Spaniards are keen on words with double-meanings, particularly those with a sexual innuendo. The mere mention or sight of '*huevo*' (meaning egg, but also testicle) is enough to set some people off. However, even if you have a good command of Spanish you may find it impossible to see what's funny – and this may be because to you it simply isn't funny.

The Spanish like 'in-your face' humour with a large dose of exaggeration – caricature, imitation

of famous people, ridiculous disguises (think huge glasses, wild wigs and enormous false bosoms) and absurd situations all form part of a 'good laugh'. Comedy shows on TV consist mainly of parody – Spanish housewives, mothers-in-law and pensioners are often the main characters – as well as caricatures of politicians, singers and the latest famous faces. In recent years, stand-up comedy has become increasingly popular, although this more subtle and 'intellectual' form of comedy is confined to small venues and late-night TV viewing.

The Spanish also like crude humour (*humor verde* – 'green humour', not blue) – jokes are usually frank and leave little to the imagination. This may come as a surprise considering the deep religious background of many people. And rude-joke telling isn't confined to men-only bars: even older people indulge in it, 'jokes' often involving graphic detail. If this is the case, try not to be embarrassed; the joke-teller won't be.

Regional stereotypes also feature strongly in Spanish jokes, e.g. supposed Catalan stinginess, Basque virility and Andalusian backwardness. The inhabitants of the strawberry-growing town of Lepe in Huelva (Andalusia) are Spain's answer to the Irish (for the British) or the Belgians (for the French) and there are literally thousands of jokes involving the stupidity of the hapless *Leperos*. For example: 'Why do the people from Lepe wear nets on their heads? So their ideas can't escape.' When the Spanish as a people feature in a joke it's usually to highlight their *joie de vivre* and spontaneity at the cost of the (relatively) staid or rigid attitudes of other peoples.

> At the top of Spain's class system sits the Duchess of Alba, who has so many titles after her name that (as Spaniards frequently tell you) the Queen of England would have to curtsey to her and not the other way round.

Joke telling is an art in Spain (as it is elsewhere) and until you feel completely at home with the language and the people, it's probably best to listen to jokes rather than tell them. Above all, don't bother to translate jokes from your home country into Spanish: the language rarely works and even if it does, the chances are that the listeners won't find it funny.

THE CLASS SYSTEM

At first glance Spain doesn't appear to have a class system and any Spaniard will happily tell you that there's little class division within Spanish society. It certainly isn't as clearly defined as the British or even French class systems and cannot be discerned from someone's accent (as in the UK). But scratch the surface and you'll discover that the class system is alive and kicking.

The Spanish class system is based on the (comforting?) fact that there's always someone 'below' you and its structure is basically as follows. At the top are Spain's 400 or so aristocrats, known as *Grandes de España*, many of whom are occasionally forced to pose for extensive spreads in *Hola* magazine to make ends meet, but who nevertheless still have considerable social cachet. Then come numerous minor nobles (also obliged to pose for *Hola*, but more often) with multi-barrelled surnames, and the owners of decaying castles around Spain. Under these are middle-class professionals, a status that numerous Spaniards aspire to – professionals in suits receive widespread deference and 'top dogs' such as notaries are almost revered.

Next in the pecking order are white-collar, blue-collar and agricultural workers. Assorted foreigners follow (few make it further up the class ladder unless they marry a Spaniard) with drunken, shell suit-wearing tourists seen as the lowest of the low – except for Spain's 650,000 gypsies, who lie at the bottom of the class heap. Gypsies are treated as lepers by many Spaniards (except when they're celebrated flamenco artists, e.g. Joaquín Cortés, or bullfighters).

CHILDREN

Most Spanish families are now small units and no longer have at least four children as was common during the '60s and '70s, and many have only one child despite government incentives for couples to produce three or more children (*familia numerosa*). However, children still have a privileged place in Spanish society (it's common to see an adoring group of adults around a pushchair or pram cooing over a small child). They're pampered from birth, and youngsters are often immaculately dressed in expensive outfits and patent shoes. They're showered with gifts at Epiphany, birthdays and their first communion.

Children are seen **and** heard in Spain, where noisy play and shouting is permitted almost everywhere and rarely reprimanded. They're encouraged to take part in social activities and stay up much later than many of their European counterparts; on summer evenings it's common to see children playing outside until at least midnight. Children are welcome in the vast majority of bars, cafés and restaurants (only the most exclusive refuse entry to under 18s), and many eateries offer children's menus and provide high chairs, balloons and colouring books and pencils.

Children are generally polite and considerate, and there's little 'yob' culture in Spanish society. Teenagers go out with their parents at weekends and join in family holidays, and most value the family unit highly. Leaving home isn't a priority for most children and many continue to live with their parents until they're 30. High property prices are partly the cause of this, but even young adults who can afford to often don't leave their parents' home until they get married. Children who work and live at home aren't usually expected to contribute to the family finances and continue to be pampered well into adulthood.

ATTITUDES TO FOREIGNERS

In today's turbulent times, with religious tension and strife at the forefront of the world's problems, it's difficult to believe that for several centuries three of the world's main religious groups (Christians, Jews and Muslims) lived in almost uninterrupted racial harmony in much of Spain. The Catholic Reconquest, completed by Isabel and Ferdinand in 1492, put an end to this and all Jews and Muslims were expelled from Spain or forced to convert to Catholicism. For centuries afterwards, acute national poverty meant that Spain was a country of emigrants – thousands left for Central and South America, or Europe during Franco's dictatorship – and few foreigners arrived. As a result, the Spanish population was until comparatively recently almost all Spanish-born, white and Catholic, and Spaniards were relatively unused to foreigners, with little direct experience of other cultures and ways of life. This began to change with the advent of package tourism heralding the arrival of the first foreign residents in the '70s and particularly during the '90s economic boom, which prompted mass immigration to Spain from Central and South America and Africa, particularly Morocco.

> Although comparatively few Spaniards have read Don Quixote in its entirety, almost everyone can recite the opening line: En un lugar de La Mancha de cuyo nombre no quiero recordarme, no ha mucho tiempo vivía un hidalgo... (In a place in La Mancha whose name I have no wish to remember there once lived a knight...).

Just as Spaniards claim not to have any class prejudice, they will tell you that they aren't racist or xenophobic. However, although this is generally true, xenophobia is on the increase as a rising tide of immigrants washes the country's shores – in a nationwide survey in October 2006, Spaniards cited immigration as their principal concern, ahead of unemployment, terrorism and lack of affordable housing. Some equate immigration with delinquency and would happily eject all gypsies, Romanians and North Africans from Spain. National campaigns remind Spaniards that immigrant workers' contributions to the social security system account for a significant part of its current buoyant pension fund and highlight the cultural richness of immigrants. However, sociologists express the concern that little is being done to educate Spaniards about their new neighbours, and some experts worry that within a couple of decades Spanish society will suffer from the same racial tensions as France and the UK.

While the Spanish aren't as blatantly derogatory about other nationalities as, say, the British, their language includes a number of less-than-complimentary references to foreigners, including the following:

- *cabeza de turco* (Turk's head) – a scapegoat
- *despedirse a la francesa* (say goodbye the French way) – to leave without saying goodbye
- *hacerse el sueco* (to pretend to be Swedish) – to act stupid.
- *merienda de negros* (black people's afternoon tea) – a chaotic occasion
- *un cuento chino* (a Chinese story) – a fictitious tale

NATIONAL ICONS

Every country boasts its icons – people, places, food (and drink) and symbols – that are unique to its culture and have special significance to its inhabitants. Spain is, of course, no exception. The following is a list of the principal icons of Spanish culture – to which you can expect to come across almost daily reference.

Icons – People

Pedro Almodóvar (b 1951) – One of Europe's top film directors,

whose latest films have received the highest accolades, including an Oscar. Almodóvar's films focus on women and sexuality and feature quintessentially Spanish backdrops dominated by religion, folklore and popular culture. Almodóvar is responsible for launching the careers of numerous Spanish actors, including Antonio Banderas and Penelope Cruz (see below).

Fernando Alonso (b 1981) – A recent arrival on the Spanish icon scene, Alonso already has millions of fans – particularly in Asturias, his homeland – on account of his double world title in Formula 1 racing in 2005 and 2006. Alonso also appears frequently in TV advertisements and his engagement to Raquel del Rosario, lead singer in El Sueño de Morfeo (a top pop group), adds to his celebrity status.

Bullfighters

Too many are famous and nationally revered for them all to be mentioned here, but among the most iconic are Belmonte (1892-1962), considered to be the greatest ever; Dominguín (1926-1998), who retired after a serious goring; Paquirri (1948-84), one of the best contemporary fighters, but fatally gored at a fight; and El Cordobés (b. 1938), responsible for making bullfighting a popular 'sport'.

Antonio Banderas (b 1960) – Known as Spain's most popular export, Banderas was the first actor to triumph in Hollywood. Married to Melanie Griffith, he has acted in scores of films and recently started directing. He promotes Spain

(particularly Malaga, his home town) wherever he goes.

Penelope Cruz (1974) – Another of Spain's best-known exports to Hollywood, although her acting is rated far more highly in Europe than across the Pond. She's frequently voted as one of the world's most beautiful women and is the only Spanish actress to have been nominated for an Oscar.

Salvador Dalí (1904-89) – Known for his dreamscapes, dripping clocks and quirky moustache, Salvador Dalí was one of the world's most prolific exponents of Surrealism. His house-museum at Cadaqués – complete with giant egg sculpture on the roof – and the Theatre-Museum at Figueres housing 1,500 of his works are among Spain's most-visited museums.

Lola Flores (1923-95) – Known as 'Lola de España' and 'La Faraona', Lola Flores is Spain's most famous folklore icon. She had a long music and cinema career as an actress, flamenco singer and dancer.

Pau Gasol (b 1980) – One of Spain's tallest men as well as a top basketball player, Gasol was the first Spanish player to join the US NBA league. He's also the captain of the national team and led them to victory in the 2006 World Championships.

Julio Iglesias (b 1943) – One of the world's most famous crooners and the idol of many a housewife during the '70s and '80s. Thirty years later, Julio's still going strong in more ways than vocally – his tenth child is about to be born.

Miguel Induráin (b 1964) – The country's greatest and one of the world's top cyclists, Induráin won the Tour de France five times in succession from 1991 to 1995.

Federico García Lorca (1898-36) – Lorca is one of Spain's best known poets and playwrights. His prolific career ended abruptly when he was shot by Nationalist forces at the start of the Civil War. His most famous works include the plays *The House of Bernarda Alba* and *Blood Wedding* and the abstract verse in his collection of poetry *Poet in New York*.

Mortadelo y Filemón – Spain's best-loved cartoon duo, whose misadventures drawn by Francisco Ibáñez have been featuring in comics since 1958. A film of their antics was a major box-office success in 2003.

Pablo Picasso (1881-1973) – Although Pablo Ruiz Picasso is Spain's most famous painter and probably its most universal, he only lived in Spain for the first 23 years of his life. His birthplace, Malaga, has two museums dedicated to his work and Barcelona, where he lived before emigrating to France, is home to one of the world's top Picasso collections.

Don Quixote – The hero of the world's first novel (written in 1605 by Miguel de Cervantes), Don Quixote encompasses the best and worst of the traditional Spanish character. His faithful servant Sancho Panza, decrepit horse Rocinante and ladylove Dulcinea are also household names.

Raúl (b 1977) – Captain of Real Madrid and the national football team, Raúl González (known by his first name only) is Spain's highest-ever goal scorer.

Arantxa Sánchez Vicario (b 1971) – Spain's top female tennis player, several times winner of Roland Garros (the French Open) and Olympic medals and a key doubles player, Vicario retired in 2002.

Manolo Santana (b 1938) – Spain's first Roland Garros winner (he won it in 1961 and 1964) and Spain's only winner of Wimbledon (1966).

Adolfo Suárez (b 1932) – One of the key players in Spain's transition to democracy and the country's first democratically elected president after 1975. He's known for his negotiating skills and moderate views at a time when political tension ran high.

Don Juan Tenorio – The archetype of the male seducer, Don Juan is a character from a Tirso de Molina play who supposedly reflects the character of Spanish men.

> **Ñ** – Spanish is the only major language to use the letter ñ and it's so much a part of the culture – the official Spanish cultural institute abroad, the Instituto Cervantes, uses ñ as a symbol for cultural heritage – that even España cannot do without it.

Icons – Places

Camino de Santiago – The 'Way of Saint James' to the cathedral of Santiago de Compostela in Galicia, where the saint's body is supposedly buried, has been one of the most important Christian pilgrimages since medieval times. There is in fact no single 'way', although a few routes are considered the main ones. The most popular route, known as the French route (*Ruta Francesa*), runs from Le Puy in France across northern Spain, and is trudged by thousands of walkers, cyclists and horse riders every year. The Camino's symbol is a large scallop shell (*concha de peregrino*), which pilgrims wear on

necklaces or attached to walking sticks.

Cibeles – The fountain topped with the pagan goddess of earth and fertility in her chariot pulled by two lions is Madrid's most famous monument and sits at the entrance to the Paseo del Prado. Major sporting victories, including those by Real Madrid, are celebrated around (and in) the fountain. Doñana – Of all Spain's many national parks, this is her most prized possession and also Europe's largest nature reserve. Its extensive marshes and dunes are home to dozens of species of birds including the rare Spanish imperial eagle and flamingos as well as numerous mammals such as the endangered lynx – of which a mere two dozen survive.

Guernica – This small Basque town was razed by Nazi bombing in 1937 – a foretaste of what was to happen to so many towns and cities in subsequent wars. Picasso's painting of the event is one of the world's most famous and a national treasure, housed in Madrid's Reina Sofía museum.

Teide – Spain's highest peak and the Canaries' sole icon (at least in this list). In an island group where the sun shines for most of the year and the average annual temperature is around 24C, it's surprising to discover that the Teide's summit is often snow-capped.

Icons – Symbols

Bull – Icon of the *fiesta nacional* (the bull fight), essential ingredient in many local fiestas and popularly claimed to represent the Spaniards' impetuous, fiery nature, the black fighting bull (*toro bravo*) adorns tacky souvenirs, car stickers and T-shirts, and giant bull silhouettes (the symbol of Osbourne sherry) dominate the highways and are national monuments.

Carnation – Spain's national flower, carnations (*claveles* – almost always red or white) are worn in buttonholes, grown on balconies, thrown as a sign of appreciation (at parades and concerts) and woven into funeral wreaths.

Castanets – Along with the guitar, castanets (*castañuelas*) are a vital component of Spanish music and played with all fingers and both hands.

El Corte Inglés – Spain's flagship department store was originally a children's clothing shop, founded in Madrid in 1890. The first 'department' store (on just two floors) opened in 1940 and since then the company has opened dozens

of stores and hypermarkets all over Spain. Prices are high, but goods are of high quality and customer service is excellent. It also must be the only store in the world to send its cardholders a Christmas and birthday card.

Flamenco – Originating in the south but referred to as the soul of Spain, flamenco (singing, dancing and music) is an essential part of the country's culture and traditions. Its most famous figures include Camerón de la Isla (singer), Paco de Lucía (guitar) and Antonio Ruiz Soler (dancer).

Goyas – Spain's equivalent of the Oscars and BAFTAs, these 28 highly coveted busts of the painter Goya are awarded to the *crème de la crème* of the Spanish film industry every year.

Hola – One of Spain's top-selling weekly gossip magazines – of which there are many – and a pioneer of the genre, *Hola* was first published in 1944; each issue focuses on the glitzy and respectable sides of show business and aristocratic life.

SEAT – Originally an affiliate of Fiat, SEAT is now part of the VW group but still **the** Spanish car company. The tiny SEAT 600 was the first car to make a major impact on Spaniards' lives and became a symbol of new wealth in the '60s. These tiny cars are now collectors' items and proudly paraded on Spanish roads – but usually with only two passengers instead of whole families of six or eight, who used to cram in.

Zara – The Galician fashion empire created by Amancio Ortega – famous for being Spain's richest person (and 23rd in the world) and for never giving interviews or having his photograph in the media – is one of the world's most successful businesses with an annual turnover of nearly €5bn and 450 stores in 29 countries. The secret of its success apparently lies in Zara's ability to copy what's on the catwalks and have it in the stores within two weeks.

Zarzuela – A Spanish musical genre similar to operetta, although with more dialogue. The first *zarzuelas* appeared in the 17th century and reached the height of their popularity in late 19th. *Zarzuelas* are regularly performed throughout Spain, among the most famous being 'Agua, azucarillos y aguardiente', 'Las Verónicas' and 'La Verbena de la Paloma'.

Icons – Food & Drink

Casera – Spain's own fizzy drink (lemonade) that continues to top sales in spite of fierce competition from Coca-Cola, Fanta and Schweppes. A typical summer drink is a '*tinto de verano*' – red wine mixed with Casera and served with lemon and ice.

Chupa Chups – One of Spain's best known exports, a Chupa Chups lollipop is reportedly sold every minute somewhere in the world. Dalí designed the daisy logo on the wrapper that now encases one of 40 flavours.

Churros – Deep-fried dough sticks – some thick and others thin, but all highly-calorific – *churros* are the ultimate comfort food when partnered by a thick hot chocolate drink, especially on a cold winter's afternoon or after a night on the tiles.

Cola Cao – A rich cocoa powder that when mixed with hot milk forms part of every Spanish child's

(and many adults') breakfast and *merienda* (afternoon snack). The distinctive round yellow tins have been around since 1946 and more than 40m kilos of *Cola Cao* (which, strictly, is a brand name) are sold every year.

Ensaimada – A large, round and typically Mallorcan pastry, sometimes filled with pumpkin conserve (*cabello de ángel* – angel hair) and packed in outsize octagonal boxes. In 2006, the airport authorities revised EU security directives so that that holidaymakers flying out of Mallorca could carry *ensaimadas* as hand luggage.

Paella – The Spanish dish (as well as the only one every Spanish man can cook). Traditional *paella*, originally from Valencia, contains rabbit and green beans, but nowadays anything goes: chicken, pork, fish, shellfish, squid, peppers, peas…

Rioja – The best known of all the Spanish wine-growing areas and the country's most famous red (*tinto*), high in tannin and often with a distinctive oaky flavour from the barrels. Many connoisseurs believe that vintage Rioja wines can hold their own with the best France has to offer (which pleases the Spanish immensely).

Tortilla – A Spanish tortilla is an omelette. At the annual search for Spain's best *tortilla*, the winner always contains onion (*cebolla*), but authentic *tortilla* is made from potato slices and eggs only. Most bars offer *tortilla* as a *tapa* and it's a picnic staple. All-egg omelette is known as 'French omelette' (*tortilla francesa*).

Turrones, mazapanes & mantecados – Traditional Christmas fare. There are two sorts of *turrón*: Alicante (a hard, white slab made with whole almonds) and Jijona (a smooth, soft slab made with ground almonds). *Mazapán* (a fine, almost white marzipan) is modelled into figurines and the best is made in Toledo. *Mantecados* (a type of pastry made with flour, lard and spices) come in small (and heavy) individual packets that you need to squeeze tightly before opening so that the contents don't disintegrate all over you; Antequera and Estepa (both in Andalusia) reportedly make the best.

Ronda, Andalucia

3.
GETTING STARTED

One of the most difficult stages of adjustment to a new country is those first few days when you have a million and one things to do. This is stressful enough without the addition of cultural differences. This chapter will help you overcome the challenges of arriving and settling in Spain, including those posed by obtaining a residence permit, finding accommodation, renting or buying a car, opening a bank account, registering for taxes, obtaining healthcare, council services and utilities, finding schools for your children, getting online and staying informed – and Spanish bureaucracy.

> Most foreigners have a tale to tell about their dealings with Spanish officialdom and not all tales have a happy ending..

IMMIGRATION

If you're white and an EU national, getting through immigration controls when you arrive in Spain is usually straightforward. If you aren't white and/or are from a country outside the EU, expect the procedure to take longer – your passport and visa will be thoroughly checked and stamped and your luggage possibly searched.

Young travellers with an 'unusual' appearance are almost always searched and questioned, as are visitors from 'exotic' regions, e.g. Africa, South America (particularly Colombia), and the Middle and Far East, who may find themselves under scrutiny from customs officials seeking illegal drugs.

Immigration officials (national police) and customs officers (civil guards) are generally polite, but the bonus is on you to prove your

bona fides and you should remain calm and civil, however long the entry procedure takes.

BUREAUCRACY

One of the few topics that the Spanish and foreigners in Spain are unanimous on is that bureaucracy places obstacles in the way of everyday life. 'Red tape' in Spain is omnipresent and one of the most pernicious in the Western world and all foreigners (unless they're tourists) will inevitably come up against the (very thick) wall of Spanish bureaucracy. The authorities love paperwork and even the simplest application requires a profusion of forms, certificates and photocopies.

Anecdotes of hopeless wandering

Residence Cards

Not necessary for EEA and Swiss nationals who are employees, self-employed or full-time students, but many people have found that, in practice, it's useful to have a residence permit for identification purposes (it's considerably smaller than a passport), particularly British citizens who don't have a national identity card. Some transactions (e.g. opening a resident's bank account or applying for a mortgage) still require proof of residence, usually in the form of a residence card.

Necessary for EEA nationals who are retired (or non-working) and all non-EEA nationals; must be applied for within a month of arrival.

A residence card can be obtained from your nearest police station, where you must present proof of identity and status in Spain (e.g. a salary slip, student card or social security documentation). Cards are issued fairly quickly – within a few days in some cases.

you can apply online in some cases. The government has also established 'one-stop' offices (*ventanilla única*) where all information and documentation is available and you can present everything relevant to your application. Businesses (the number of documents required to set up a business is astronomical) are particularly well catered for.

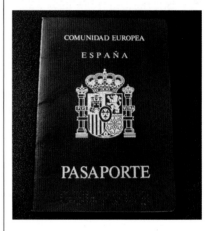

These offices are available in all provinces (☎ 902 100 096, 🖳 www.ventanillaempresarial. org). There are plenty of other information sources, such as town halls (those with foreigners' departments are especially helpful), expatriate support groups and local chambers of commerce (*cámara de comercio*). In spite of these improvements, many applications still take 'for ever' to be resolved, civil servants occasionally change the required documentation and you almost always have to queue.

from one office to another and days spent queuing, only to be told that the required documentation has changed or that the only civil servant authorised to deal with your case is off sick, are commonplace. Stories abound of applications that took months or even years.

However, in recent years, successive governments have made efforts to reduce the paperwork and streamline many application processes. The advent of the internet has helped considerably; not only can you consult lists of required documents on official websites but

Many foreigners find the red tape impenetrable, especially if they don't speak Spanish, and it's said that when you come up against the full force of Spanish bureaucracy you understand what it **really** means to be a foreigner.

Top tips for dealing with Spanish red tape:

- Always find out from an official source beforehand **exactly** what you need.
- Double-check the opening hours of the office and ensure it isn't a public holiday (national, regional or local).
- Always take a duplicate of everything.
- Expect not to have the right paperwork the first time (no one ever does).
- Allow most of the morning to make an application (and take a good book).

If you don't have a reasonable command of Spanish or your patience is thin, there are ways to get round the red tape (see **Getting Round Bureaucracy** below). However, it's best to accept bureaucratic hurdles as part of life in Spain and remember that Spaniards have to go through the same process.

Civil Servants

Spanish civil servants are an institution in themselves and there are thousands of them – teachers, policemen, forest rangers and post office workers as well as employees in government offices. For decades, becoming a civil servant in Spain has meant a job for life (it's almost impossible to be dismissed if you work for the state) with working hours from 8am to 3pm

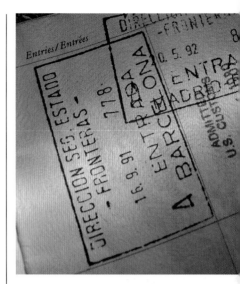

(including a mandatory half-hour coffee/breakfast break), guaranteed holidays, annual salary increases and pensions. Not surprisingly, civil service is seen as a cushy number, particularly in a country where over a third of employees are in temporary or short-term employment (the highest proportion in the EU).

The civil service exams (known as *oposiciones*) attract thousands of entrants for a few hundred places.

Many people spend years studying for the exams and there are specialist academies and private tutors all over Spain who prepare candidates.

Everyone over 13 must carry personal identification and you can be fined for not doing so. EEA nationals should carry their residence card, passport or national identity card. Non-EEA nationals should carry their residence card.

One afternoon, a man about to enter one of the ministries in Madrid is stopped by the concierge, who asks him where he's going, as there's no one in the building.
'Oh, don't they work in the afternoon?' the man asks, surprised.
'They don't work in the morning. In the afternoon they don't come in,' replies the concierge.

As a result, civil servants are perceived as holding tremendous power over the humble citizen and many Spaniards believe that an application approval sometimes depends on a civil servant's whim. Times are changing, however, and in 2006 the government announced that civil servants no longer have a 'divine right' to their jobs but must meet specified objectives. Nowadays, you're more likely to deal with a helpful civil servant than one whose mission in life is to make yours as difficult as possible, but there are still some of these around.

When dealing with civil servants, be as polite and calm as possible – you'll achieve nothing by getting angry or frustrated and the civil servant may take a dislike to you and possibly hold up your application – and always thank them for their help. They may remember your politeness and treat you well the next time.

Getting Round Bureaucracy

However good your command of Spanish and however endless your patience, it's recommended to take the following steps to mitigate the effects of Spanish bureaucracy.

Gestores

Employing a *gestor*, a licensed professional who is an expert in administrative and tax affairs and acts as a middleman between you and officialdom, is one of the most popular ways of getting round the red tape. A *gestor*'s services aren't generally expensive and most people find it money well spent.

They usually work in a *gestoría*, where there may be a number of experts dealing with different matters, including employment and residence permits, setting up a business, obtaining a driving licence or tourist plates, importing a car or paying a traffic fine, social security, and certain taxes. Ask around for recommendations as not all *gestores* can be relied upon to do a professional job, but most will save you considerable time and stress. Not for nothing do many Spaniards use the services of a *gestor*.

The maxim 'it's not what you know but who you know' applies to many situations in Spain, where calling for favours is a popular way of dealing with bureaucracy. Knowing the right person (or someone who knows the right person) at a government office or town hall often greatly facilitates an application. Officially, this practice (known as *enchufismo* – literally 'plugging in') is frowned on and often deplored, but in practice it's commonly used to oil the wheels of Spanish bureaucracy. If you find that an application is taking longer than usual, there's no harm in seeing if you or a friend has a contact in the department you're applying to.

> It's estimated that just 11 per cent of housing in Spain is rented accommodation, although there are huge regional variations – Madrid has 16 per cent and Barcelona 28 per cent. In these two cities, the average annual rental is €9,600.

ACCOMMODATION

Finding suitable accommodation is one of your first and most important tasks on arrival in Spain – but it isn't always plain sailing.

Rented Property

Some landlords in Spain refuse to let their property to tenants of certain nationalities and/or skin colours. It isn't unheard of for a prospective tenant to arrange a meeting with a landlord by phone but to have the door shut in his face once the landlord sees that the tenant isn't white. This attitude is more common outside cities but rears its ugly head everywhere. There's little you can do about it other than carry on looking in the hope of finding a 'tolerant' landlord.

Some landlords are reluctant to let to **any** foreigners – stories of foreign tenants who disappear owing months' rent are common – so don't be surprised if a landlord asks to see your residence card and stipulates that you provide a guarantor (a third party who commits himself to paying your rent if you don't) or a bank guarantee (whereby, in the case of non-payment by the tenant, the bank takes over payment on the tenant's behalf).

Contracts & Payment

It's worth signing a rental contract, not only for your peace of mind but also because Spanish rental law is more than generous to tenants. If you sign a long-term contract (*contrato de arrendamiento*), you have the right to occupy a property for a minimum of five years (irrespective of the dates stated in the contract) and can exercise first right to buy the

property should the landlord decide to sell it.

Many landlords in Spain don't declare their rental income to the tax authorities and are therefore reluctant to sign a rental contract with tenants. Don't be tempted to rent a property without a proper contract because, although it seems an easy option with no strings attached, you'll have no rights and the landlord no obligations. There are also potential problems with insurance. The landlord might claim that his 'word' is as good as a contract (under Spanish law, oral agreements are considered legal), but in a possible court case it would be your word against the landlord's.

Don't make any monthly payments in cash without obtaining a receipt. If you pay via a bank (e.g. direct debit or transfer), the transaction serves as proof of payment.

Landlords

Spanish landlords are no better and no worse than those in other countries – which means that yours could be honest or crooked. Some people find that properties managed by a letting company rather than an individual landlord are better maintained and repairs carried out more quickly, but others discover that letting companies are often too busy to arrange maintenance.

Whether your contact is a landlord or a company, try to keep in their good books by keeping the accommodation in good order and abiding by community rules and regulations: tenants aren't permitted to sub-let a property without the landlord's permission, carry out any improvements or repairs, cause a nuisance to neighbours or carry out any dangerous activity in the property. As a good tenant you'll have more chance of getting things done than someone who isn't looking after the property or has been complained about. Ask firmly but politely for anything you need done and remember that this is Spain and you might have to ask several times before anything happens.

Buying a Home

Property purchase in Spain is generally a straightforward process, but you may be surprised by the following aspects of the procedure:

- Fees associated with a purchase add 10 to 12 per cent to the cost, which means that in spite of high price rises and the apparent potential for making money from buying and selling property, you need to own a house for up to three years simply to recover the associated fees.

- The first step in buying a property is to sign a contract and pay a deposit (generally 10 per cent of the price). If you don't complete the purchase, you lose the deposit but if the seller doesn't complete you get your deposit back plus the same amount again. This practice means that gazumping is almost unknown in Spain.

- Completion on a resale property takes from one to four months. Completion on a new property can take a year but usually takes longer.

- Illegal buildings aren't uncommon in Spain – experts estimate that there are between 20,000 and 30,000 in Marbella alone – and if you inadvertently buy one it could be demolished.

- If you buy a property, you're liable for any debts, charges or encumbrances left unpaid by the previous owner for up to five years after the purchase.

- You may have to pay part of the price in cash – many buyers go to the notary to complete the purchase with an envelope of banknotes.

- Apartment blocks often have paper-thin walls, so check for noisy neighbours before committing yourself.

> Don't be afraid to try out your bartering skills with a car dealer, who will often (but only if asked) lower the list price or include extras 'free'.

BUYING OR HIRING A CAR

If you live anywhere except the middle of a city, you'll almost certainly want a car. Here are a few tips on hiring (renting) and buying.

Car Hire

Hiring a car in Spain (where more visitors hire cars than in any other European country) is surprisingly cheap. To hire a car you must be over 21 years old (25 for certain cars) and most companies have an upper age limit, e.g. 65. You must show a valid driving licence (original only) – non-EU licence holders require an international driving permit – and usually personal identification as well. Payment must usually be made by credit card.

When choosing a hire car, bear in mind the summer heat (air-conditioning is a must) and the high accident rate on Spanish roads due to often appalling driving standards – try to protect yourself by hiring a robust car rather than one of the cheaper models.

Buying a Car

To buy a car in Spain you must own a property or have a rental contract (minimum one year) or be registered as a resident in your municipality (*empadronado*). Non-residents cannot buy a car on a hire purchase agreement. The paperwork involved in a car purchase is (not surprisingly) extensive and is usually handled by the dealer or a *gestor* and costs from €100.

New Cars

Most new cars are sold at list price, although you should still shop around, as dealers compete in offering discounts, guarantees, financing terms (beware of high interest rates in these) and other incentives.

Used Cars

Used car dealers have the same dreadful (and usually well deserved) reputation in Spain as in other countries, and caution must be taken when buying from them.

There are many 'cowboys' (often foreigners) selling worthless wrecks (the small advertisements in the expatriate press are full of them) and it's generally better to buy from a reputable dealer, even if you pay a bit more, and obtain a warranty,

usually valid for two years.

Right-hand Drive Cars

Unless you plan to return to the UK (or another country where driving is on the left) within a short time, importing or buying a right-hand drive car isn't a practical option.

Driving a right-hand drive car on the right-hand side of the road isn't easy and your visibility is greatly reduced, particularly when pulling out of a slip road. Numerous accidents occur every year involving right-hand drive cars – usually because they pull in front of another car they cannot 'see'.

EMERGENCY SERVICES

Spain has extremely efficient emergency services (*servicios de emergencia*) and except in remote rural areas the time between call-out and arrival is usually brief.

Spain has three police forces with separate and clearly defined functions, but you can call any in an emergency. All police carry guns and ammunition belts. Police guarding important buildings, on security alerts and at major airports carry machine-guns.

However, telephone operators rarely speak English, so be prepared to explain briefly in Spanish the type of emergency and your exact location – try to give a landmark, if possible (see **Emergency Phrases** below).

Emergency Numbers

The main national emergency numbers are as follows:

No.	Service
112	All-purpose emergency number
061	Ambulance service (*ambulancia*)
062	Civil Guard (*guardia civil*)
080	Fire service (*bomberos*)
092	Local police (*policía local*)
091	National police (*policía nacional*)
900	Maritime rescue (*salvamento y seguridad marítimo*)

Emergency Phrases

accident (car) – *accidente* (*de coche*)
allergic reaction – *reacción alérgica*
attack (armed) – *ataque* (*con arma*)
bleeding (a lot) – *sangrando* (*mucho*)
broken arm – *brazo roto*
broken leg – *pierna rota*
burglary – *robo en casa*
fire – *fuego* or *incendio*
heart attack – *infarto* or *paro cardiaco*
I need an ambulance – *necesito una ambulancia*
I need a doctor – *necesito un médico*
mugging – *atraco*
not breathing – *no respira*
(I am) on the road to x – (*Estoy*) *en la carretera a x*
overdose – *sobredosis*
unconscious – *inconsciente*
wounded – *herido*

HEALTH SERVICES

The World Health Organization's most recent report into worldwide health and healthcare standards (2000) found that Spain has the sixth-highest level of health and the seventh-best healthcare system in the world (the UK ranked 24 and 18 respectively). While the Spanish health service isn't without its shortcomings, most expatriate residents agree that the levels of care and expertise are excellent.

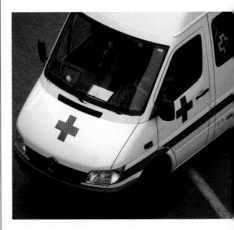

State Healthcare

Those who qualify for state healthcare include employees, the self-employed contributing to Spanish social security and EU pensioners who have reached retirement age in their home country, as well as the dependants of all these. If you qualify for state healthcare, you must register at your nearest social security office (for a list of offices see 🖳 www.seg-social. es or look in the yellow pages under *oficina de seguridad social*).

You must present proof of employment or self-employment in Spain or form E-101 or E-121, proof of residence (e.g. a property deed, rental contract or proof of registration in your municipality) and your passport. After registration you'll receive a social security card (*tarjeta de la seguridad social*), the size of a credit card, with your social security number on it. This must be presented whenever you require medical treatment. The card takes up to two months to arrive, but when you register you're issued with a temporary form proving that you've registered and are entitled to state healthcare.

Choosing a Doctor

You must usually register at your nearest health centre, but you're entitled to choose your family doctor (*médico de cabecera*) and paediatrician (*pediátrico*) for

children under 14. You'll be given a list of doctors and should base your choice on recommendations from other patients, the doctor's sex, whether the doctor speaks English, the time of his clinics and the number of patients he has – getting an appointment with a popular doctor can be difficult. If you need specialist care or hospital treatment, you're also entitled to choose who treats you and where (within your region).

> If you can choose, ask for an appointment near the start of a clinic to minimise waiting time – patients are allocated just three minutes for a consultation, but in practice most are with the doctor at least twice as long..

Getting an Appointment

Doctors' appointments can be obtained in person, by telephone and, in certain regions (e.g. Andalusia, the Canaries and Galicia), online. In all cases you need your social security card number; for online appointments you also need your residence card or passport number. Appointments are difficult to obtain by phone, as lines are often constantly engaged. With perseverance (and use of the redial button) you should eventually get through – lunchtime (e.g. 3pm) is the best time to phone – but don't expect to get an appointment the same day.

Visiting the Doctor

Arrive five or ten minutes before your appointment and check that your name is on the numbered list posted outside the surgery. It can be helpful to ask others waiting which number is currently in the surgery (*¿por qué número va?*) and to find out who has the number preceding yours (*¿quién tiene el número x?*).

Prescriptions

Prescriptions issued by social security doctors are subsidised and you pay 40 per cent of the price (the over 65s and disabled pay nothing), not a fixed amount per prescription. Some private health insurance companies reimburse this amount. There's no discount for medicine purchased without a prescription.

This gives you an idea of how slowly the clinic is going and how much time you're likely to have to wait. Don't worry about losing track of which number is in the surgery – every new arrival asks and checks which number the others have, and at least one person will keep up a running commentary on the clinic's progress.

Emergency Treatment

All state hospitals and many large health centres offer emergency treatment. Many Spaniards (and foreigners) use this facility as a way of circumnavigating the health centre system (see above) and as a result, most emergency clinics are always full to bursting point. After admittance, you're examined by a nurse who finds out how urgent your case is. Those cases deemed urgent are given priority; others are assigned to the queue, which often means a long wait by the end of which you'll be familiar with everyone else's ailments and medical history.

Despite notices asking for silence and frequent reprimands from medical staff, emergency waiting rooms are a buzz of loud conversation and mobile phone calls – the worst medicine if you're in pain.

Medicines

The Spanish are pill poppers and almost every home has a mini-pharmacy in the bathroom cabinet. A visit to the doctor usually produces two or three prescriptions for potions, tablets and ointments even for a minor ailment – not for nothing does Spain have an annual public health prescription bill of over €9.5bn. You can buy a surprising number of medicines (drugs) over the counter without a prescription, including antibiotics, which some Spaniards take routinely at the slightest sign of a common cold. Tablets aren't sold by the amount you need (e.g. for a course of antibiotics you may need eight tablets only), but by the packet – say 20 or 30, so you often end up with 'spare' medicines.

Many Spaniards claim expert medical knowledge and recommend treatments and medicines to you for just about any ailment. A recent nationwide campaign attempted to alert people to the dangers of taking medical advice from non-professionals; needless to say, many take more notice of street knowledge than their own doctor.

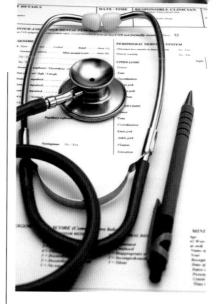

Hospitals

Public hospitals provide two- or four-bedroom wards with ensuite bathrooms and possibly a TV. In private hospitals, patients have individual rooms. Spanish patients usually receive lots of visitors (mainly relatives) so shared rooms can be noisy during visiting hours, but on the plus side the same visitors will probably 'adopt' you and share conversation and gifts, making a hospital stay less bleak if you're on your own in Spain. Close relatives and friends often spend the night with a patient – this is what the reclining chairs in all rooms are for. Towels are usually provided, but patients are expected to take pyjamas, robes and toiletries. Food is usually reasonable and many hospitals offer a choice of menus at lunchtime. You may have to provide

crutches and wheelchairs yourself (you can hire them from orthopaedic shops), although some hospitals rent them to patients.

Nursing Care

Spanish nurses are highly qualified professionals and perform many skilled jobs that their counterparts in other European countries (e.g. the UK) aren't permitted to. You may, however, find nursing care cold and impersonal, and nurses matter-of-fact rather than sympathetic. Family members provide a lot of basic nursing care in hospitals, such as feeding and helping patients back on their feet.

Medical Procedures

Medical professionals are held in awe in Spain and their recommendations and directives are followed to the letter. The concept of patient rights is a relatively new one in Spain, where the patient is expected to do as the doctor says – no questions asked. If your treatment includes scans, blood tests or other routine medical tests, don't expect detailed information about the procedure – medical staff tend to expect you to take it in your stride without batting an eyelid.

Painkillers

Spanish patients are stoical about pain and tend to endure high pain levels before receiving a painkiller. You're entitled to ask for painkillers, but they may not be administered until the doctor considers that you've suffered enough.

Childbirth

Having a baby in Spain is a highly clinical experience. Ante-natal care is good – mothers are offered regular scans, blood tests, check-ups and ante-natal classes. Don't, however, expect to be offered a birth plan: home births are practically unheard of, as are water births, birthing balls, etc. In general, medical professionals are inflexible about delivery methods, birthing position and pain relief: options here start and end with an epidural – gas and air aren't

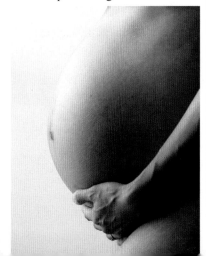

available. Partners are allowed to be present at the birth but not if it's a caesarean or there's a complication. Spain has one of the lowest infant mortality rates in the EU, but also one of the highest caesarean rates.

Post-treatment Care

Patients are expected to convalesce at home, not at hospital, and they're often discharged earlier than they would be in other countries. Don't expect home visits from doctors to check on your health or for a midwife to call after a birth – the onus is on you to go to a health centre for a check-up.

INSURANCE

Compulsory insurance policies for individuals in Spain are as follows:

- third-party insurance for car owners;
- third-party property liability insurance for homeowners and tenants;
- building insurance for mortgage holders;
- life insurance for mortgage holders.

Optional (but highly recommended) insurance policies include health, comprehensive car and car breakdown, life (unless required as above), travel and comprehensive household insurance.

Health Insurance

Even if you and your dependants qualify for state healthcare, you should ensure that you all have full health insurance during the interval between leaving your last country

Car insurance policies usually cover anyone driving the vehicle, but some policies state that the owner must give written permission to other drivers to use the car. Hire car insurance, however, only covers named drivers.

of residence and obtaining health insurance (state or private) in Spain. Spanish companies offer policies only for those living permanently in Spain and repatriation costs are rarely covered, although emergency treatment abroad is included.

Car Insurance

All motor vehicles and trailers must be insured (third-party minimum) when entering Spain. If your car is insured in an EU country, it's automatically covered for third-party liability in Spain, but if you become resident in Spain and keep a foreign-registered car, you must import it and take out a new insurance policy with a company registered in Spain. Insurance documents must be carried in the car at all times and you can be fined for not having them.

Household Insurance

A surprising number of Spaniards don't take out household insurance (*seguro de hogar*), but insuring your home and its contents is highly advisable and if you buy a property with a mortgage your bank will probably insist you have at least basic building insurance covering fire damage. Note that building insurance doesn't cover defects in a building or its design (e.g. an overweight roof that collapses) and the building must be secure, e.g. iron bars (*rejas*) on windows and reinforced windows and doors.

Contents insurance doesn't generally include objects in the garden and for high-value objects such as antiques and jewellery a separate policy is usually required. If you wish to insure your contents for more than a certain amount, e.g. €60,000, you may need to install an alarm system connected to a monitoring station.

Claims

Most companies allow claims to be made by telephone or registered letter. If you make a claim by phone, take a note of the claim reference number (you should be given one – insist if one isn't provided) and the name of the person you speak to. If the claim is for theft, insurance companies require a copy of the police report (*denuncia*), which you must make within 24 hours. If your car is stolen, the insurance company won't consider your claim until 30 days have elapsed.

Over 530,000 foreign children study in Spanish schools, accounting for around 8 per cent of the total school population, although in some areas (e.g. the Costa Blanca and Costa del Sol) the figure is over 50 per cent. More than two-fifths of foreign children study in state schools.

EDUCATION

Education is a major concern for families relocating to Spain and selecting the right sort of school for your child is one of the most difficult choices you'll face. The decision isn't one to be taken lightly and you need to spend considerable time thinking through the options and finding out as much as possible about each one. Don't forget to think beyond school to university and work, as the type of education you choose for your children has long-term implications.

Spanish or International School?

If you're able to choose between Spanish and international education, the following factors may help you to make the best choice for your child(ren).

International Schools

Spain is home to numerous international schools, although they tend to be concentrated in popular resort areas – the Costa Blanca and Costa del Sol are particularly well catered for – and in Barcelona and Madrid. An international school is ideal if your stay is short term (say up to five years) as it's less unsettling for your children if you

return to your home country or move to another country where there are international schools. Teaching methods and the language of instruction are likely to be familiar, so your children will probably adapt more quickly and easily than to a Spanish school. They won't be under pressure to learn Spanish quickly in order to understand the lessons (but make sure the school offers opportunities to learn Spanish). Standards of education are generally high and some international schools in Spain rank highly in UK IGCSE and A Level exam result tables.

Many international schools are 'melting pots' of nationalities – some have pupils from up to 50 countries – making them a unique opportunity to meet people of other cultures. In most schools in resort areas, British nationals dominate, Spaniards, Scandinavians and Germans making up the rest.

On the other hand, international schools are invariably expensive (expect to pay at least €4,000 per year for primary school, considerably more for secondary) and there's often a high turnover of pupils, relocating with their parents from one country to another. Some international schools are 'expat bubbles' and don't give children the best chance to learn the local language or mix in with the local community.

Spanish Schools

If you intend to stay in Spain long term or if you're uncertain how long you'll be there (in which case it's best to assume a long stay), a Spanish school is likely to be preferable as your child has a better chance of learning Spanish fluently. If the school is local, your children (and you) become part of the local community. Long-term education and employment possibilities are also better. Education at Spanish state schools is free and fees at private schools are considerably lower than those charged by international schools.

However, some children (particularly those over the age of ten) find schooling in Spanish academically and socially difficult.

You'll also need to learn enough Spanish to communicate with your child's teachers and understand correspondence from the school. If you live in an area where education is dominated by a regional language, this will make the situation even more difficult.

> The general level of English is low and little (if any) provision is made for native speakers, who must sit through lessons in their own language.

The Spanish Education System

Education is compulsory from 6 to 16, but most children start school at three. Education is generally of a high standard and its style and system are similar to those found in France and Italy – but totally different from those in the UK and US. The following aspects of Spanish education may surprise you:

- A lot of learning is done by rote and students are expected to memorise huge chunks of text and facts – don't be surprised to find your child having to learn all the countries in Asia and their capitals. As a result, students tend to have excellent general knowledge.

- Learning is generally teacher-orientated. Spanish education has little 'discover for yourself' learning, although this is gradually changing and some schools have introduced more autonomous, project-based work.

- All subjects have textbooks and most Spanish teachers follow

them to the letter. Even physical education (PE) may have a required textbook.

- There's little streaming in schools and most classes are mixed ability.
- Most schools have little support for non-Spanish speakers – the onus is on the student to learn Spanish as quickly as possible.
- Few Spanish teachers speak English.
- There's no national testing system (such as Key Stage testing in England) and no external examinations until the university entrance exam taken at 18 but exams are set by teachers each term.
- Students can be required to repeat a school year if they fail exams. The maximum number of years a child can repeat is one in primary and two in secondary.
- State schools don't have uniforms; private schools do.
- Many state primary schools provide lunch, but few secondary schools do. Packed lunches aren't permitted in Spanish schools

unless they're eaten during morning break.

- The school day in primary state schools usually lasts from 9am to 2pm and at secondary level from 8.30am to 1.30 or 2.30pm.
- There are generally no mid-term breaks but plenty of local/regional/national holidays, and summer holidays last between 10 and 12 weeks.
- Spanish classrooms in the state system usually have a photograph of the king on a wall. The Spanish, EU and local flags are raised on special occasions, e.g. regional day, when the regional anthem is usually sung.
- Homework isn't common in primary state schools, where teachers usually set only unfinished work or learning for a test as homework. In private primary schools, however, homework is the norm and children from the age of six have at least half an hour daily. At secondary level, state school pupils have at least two hours and private pupils around three.

Subjects

Art

- Art is largely directed and often closely follows a textbook.

Maths & Science

- Lessons are more advanced than in the UK.
- Maths involves a lot of theory learning from early on.
- A comma is used to separate whole numbers from decimals and a full stop (period) used to denote thousands, e.g. 10.000

means ten thousand.

- Children don't use a calculator in maths classes until around 13 or 14.
- Science classes tend to be more theoretical than practical.

Music

- Children learn to read music and to play the recorder and other instruments.

PE

- Teachers expect a high level of general fitness and an end of term exam may involve being able to run or swim a certain distance – students who cannot, fail the exam.

Spanish

- Spanish language learning is very grammatical – students learn the names of all grammatical terms and are expected to analyse sentences syntactically.

University

- Degree courses last at least four years.
- A high number of students take longer than the specified course length to finish their degree, e.g. six years instead of four.
- Few grants are available and no loans 'designed' for students.
- Most students go to a university in or near their home town and live at home during their studies.

> In most areas you must put your rubbish out after 9pm and you can be fined for putting it out earlier.

COUNCIL SERVICES

Refuse Collection

Unless you live in a remote rural area, refuse collections are usually daily (or nightly, as most are made in the small hours) with the exception of Sundays and public holidays.

You put your rubbish in a sealed plastic bag in a large communal container on the street or in an underground bin. If you live in an apartment block, the concierge may collect rubbish from your door. Refuse collectors take domestic rubbish only and anything else (e.g. furniture or rubble) is usually left behind. Many people dump rubbish in the countryside (the Spanish seem to have little respect for their environment), although councils impose large fines on offenders (if they catch them).

Recycling

Spain is now making a concerted effort to recycle as much as possible and in most areas there are excellent recycling facilities. However, door-to-door collection is rare and the onus is normally on you to take your recyclable materials to the appropriate place. Recycling points are plentiful and usually include blue bins (for paper, including newspapers and magazines, and cardboard), green bins (for glass), and yellow bins (for tins, plastic and cartons such as those used for milk and juice).

Some areas have introduced waste food recycling points. These are usually situated next to communal rubbish containers and identified by a fish bone symbol or the words '*basura orgánica*'. Most towns also have recycling points for batteries, clothes and cooking oil.

Other Rubbish

Computers & mobile phones: Charities in many areas collect these – ask at your council for details of collection points.

Furniture: In most areas there are weekly furniture collections, although you must usually telephone the council or community office to ask them to collect it.

Garden rubbish: Many urbanisations have collection points for garden rubbish (plant matter only).

Household goods: Charity shops operate in some areas and many charitable organisations, e.g. the Red Cross and Lux Mundi, welcome donations of unwanted goods in reasonable condition. Ask at your council or community office for details.

Medicines: Out-of-date or unwanted medicines should be taken to a chemist's – most have collection points.

Rubble: It's an offence to tip any building material anywhere other than designated tips, where there's a charge – hence the large piles of rubble dotting the Spanish countryside – and no other rubbish can be disposed of. If you have a large amount of rubble, consider hiring a skip.

UTILITIES

Arrangements for the connection and supply of power and other services aren't always straightforward. Here's a summary of the main points to look out for.

Electricity

In spite of the liberalisation of the energy market in 2003, there's still no choice of electricity supplier outside the large cities.

Supply Problems

Power cuts are frequent in many areas of Spain, although the situation is improving as companies gradually invest in more modern infrastructure. However, bad weather often makes the electricity supply unstable, with frequent power cuts lasting from less than a second (just long enough

to crash a computer) to a few hours (or days). If you live in an area where cuts are frequent and rely on electricity for your livelihood, e.g. for operating a computer, you may need to install a back-up generator.

Power surges occur occasionally and you may wish to install a power surge protector for appliances such as TVs, computers and fax machines, without which you risk having equipment damaged or destroyed. Electricity companies pay compensation for power surge damage, but it's up to you to claim it – and you still suffer the inconvenience of having equipment repaired.

If the power keeps tripping off when you attempt to use a number of high-power appliances simultaneously, e.g. an electric kettle and a heater, it means that the power rating (*potencia*) of your property is too low. This is a common problem in Spain and may be solved if you upgrade the power supply.

Water

Water is a precious commodity in Spain, where people have only recently woken up to water conservation. The drought of 2005-06, during which reservoirs in the south and south-east of Spain all but dried up, highlighted the scarcity of water and the need to save as much as possible, and there are frequent reminders in the media. In late 2006 the government announced the introduction of higher water charges for households using over 60 litres per person per day. Water is usually provided by a local company or the council and there's no choice of provider. Bills are usually quarterly and include 7 per cent VAT (*IVA*).

> If you have a complaint about a telephone service, go to your nearest consumers' office and report it. It will usually be resolved reasonably quickly and efficiently. The Ministry of Industry runs an office for telephone services complaints, open from 9am to 7pm Mondays to Fridays and 9am to 2pm on Saturdays (☎ 901 336 699, 💻 www.usuariosteleco.es).

Quality

Water is supposedly safe to drink in all urban and most rural areas, although it can be of poor quality and taste awful, particularly if it comes from a desalination plant. Many people prefer to drink bottled water.

Telephone

Telephone services are generally good and most of the country is served by landline and/or mobile phone infrastructure.

Installation

Telefónica is currently the only company that can install a telephone line – phone ☎ 1004 (in Spanish) or ☎ 902 118 247 (in English), fill out a form online (💻 www.telefonica.es or 💻 www.telefonicainenglish.com) or visit a Telefónica shop (situated in large towns and cities). Telephone installation takes up to a week in urban areas (considerably longer in rural areas) and costs around €110. Bills are sent out monthly and can be paid by direct debit or at banks.

Dealing with Telephone Companies

Spain's telephony services have been liberalised and many companies now offer line rental, calls and internet connection. There's huge competition for your custom so shop around and choose a company with the lowest rates for the type of calls you make. Be aware that rates for calls may not be consistently low in the same company and that many companies have aggressive marketing campaigns with cheap offers which often vanish into thin air the minute you sign up. Customer services leave a lot to be desired in many telephone companies and making a complaint can be time-consuming and frustrating: one of the most exasperating aspects is that it's almost impossible to speak to the same person more than once so you have to continually re-explain your problem. Almost everyone has a tale to tell about Telefónica's poor service, but other companies are no better. Telephone and internet services account for a large percentage of all consumer complaints, with over-charging and subsequent slow refunds, unannounced tariff changes, slow internet connection and the difficulty in terminating a contract at the top of the grievances list. New legislation has improved matters and companies are now obliged to provide customers with a complaint reference number and, if the customer requests it, terminate a contract within 15 days of notification.

STAYING INFORMED

Even if your knowledge of Spanish is good enough to follow Spanish

> A 2006 nationwide survey found that 70 per cent of Spanish children watch around 150 minutes of TV every day and that over 25 per cent are still watching TV at midnight.

media, you may occasionally (or often) hanker after some TV, radio or press in your own language. The good news is that this is relatively easy to obtain in Spain, particularly for English speakers.

Television

Spanish TV isn't renowned for its quality, although it's generally no worse than what's on offer in other countries and there's no licence so at least you don't have to pay for the rubbish. Programmes generally consist of game shows, chat shows, gossip shows and 'reality' shows (demonstrating the Spaniards' seemingly insatiable interest in other people's lives), and sports, although football accounts for at least 75 per cent of sport on TV. Most foreign films are dubbed into Spanish. All channels carry advertising (12 minutes per hour is permitted) and programmes are continually interrupted by adverts, which are often broadcast at a higher volume than the programme itself.

Life is shown 'warts and all' on Spanish TV, where news bulletins throughout the day broadcast close-ups of bomb damage, corpses, blood-spattered pavements, etc. Only occasionally does a newscaster warn you before particularly gory footage is shown; expect to be shocked almost daily. Adult (over 18) films and explicit sex scenes are shown only after 10pm, but films unsuitable for young children and torrid soaps are often on in the afternoon. Other than a few 'home-grown' shows such as *Los Lunnis*, children's programming consists mainly of imported cartoons (mostly American and Japanese). If you have young children, watch TV with them and have the remote control **very** close by.

> Goals scored in football are 'sung' by radio commentators, whose shout of 'gooooooooal' can go on for ever (longer if Spain has scored a goal).

There are no English-language channels broadcasting in Spain and your only option is satellite TV – many parts of Spain can receive over 200 satellite stations broadcasting in a variety of languages. The choice includes Astra satellites (🖥 www. astra.lu), BBC (🖥 www.bbcworld. com and 🖥 www.bbcprime.com), Eutelsat (🖥 www.eutelsat.org) and Sky (🖥 www.sky.com). There are many satellite sales and installation companies. Shop around and compare prices and services. Before paying for a satellite dish, however, check whether you need permission from your landlord, community (if you live in an apartment block) or council. Some areas have strict regulations regarding the size and location of dishes.

Radio

The Spanish are avid radio listeners and the quality of radio programmes is generally high. The main national stations are SER (consistently top of the audience ratings), Radio Nacional de España (Rne), COPE (owned by the Catholic church and openly highly critical of the Socialist government), Onda Cero and Punto Radio. Most broadcast a 'magazine' programme from around 7am to 1pm, including analysis of current affairs by experts, most of whom talk (or shout) at once during the so-called discussions (*tertulias*). Important sports matches are broadcast live – when you can follow a football or basketball match commentary on the radio, you've become a native.

Many stations broadcast round-the-clock pop music, e.g. Los 40 Principales (the latest on the pop scene), Kiss FM (mostly romantic and easy-listening pop music), M80 (music from the '70s to '90s) and Cadena Dial (Spanish pop music).

All stations carry advertising, which is often highly intrusive and interrupts news items and football matches.

English and other foreign-language radio stations are available only on the Costa Blanca, Costa de Almería and Costa del Sol and in the Canaries. Programmes and channels are published in the foreign-language press. The BBC World Service is broadcast on short wave on several frequencies simultaneously and you can usually receive a good signal on one of them. The Astra satellite also receives the BBC World Service. If you have cable or digital TV you should be able to receive foreign-language radio stations.

Press

Reading a newspaper is largely a middle-class habit in Spain and there's no popular tabloid or 'gutter' press (TV gossip shows more than compensate). Only one in five Spaniards buys a newspaper and only ten newspapers sell over 100,000 copies daily (four of them are sports papers). Newspapers cost €1 (€2 at weekends) and most publish free supplements covering entertainment, IT, travel, art and literature. Most newspapers have free online editions, although you need to subscribe to some to access all archives, e.g. *El País*.

Spain's main national newspapers are:

● *El País* – the best seller, founded in 1975. Editorial is left-wing and *El País* is generally recognised as the newspaper that 'taught' Spaniards the democratic process after the dictatorship.

- *El Mundo* – the second-highest seller, founded in 1990. Editorial is right-wing and the newspaper specialises in investigative journalism and virulent attacks on all political parties except the PP.
- *ABC* – the third-best selling and Spain's oldest national. Editorial is right-wing, conservative and monarchist.

The Catalan newspapers *La Vanguardia* and *El Periódico de Catalunya* are both in the top ten best sellers. Spain also has numerous regional and provincial dailies, while free daily papers such as *ADN*, *Qué* and *20 Minutos*, consisting of a 10- to 20-page news round-up, are common in towns and cities and distributed on public transport.

Many foreign newspapers are available in main cities and resort areas by the afternoon of the publication date or the following morning, and a number of British newspapers (e.g. the *Daily Mail*, *The Guardian* and *The Times*) are printed in Spain and available on the

morning of publication. Foreign newspapers cost around three times the price in their country of origin – even if they're printed locally. Many English-language newspapers and magazines are published in Spain. Most are weekly and contain

summaries of local, national and British news plus information about local events and services. Many are free. In some resort areas, other newspapers and magazines are published in Danish, French, German and Swedish.

Spain's Most-read Media (in November 2006)	
Pronto – weekly gossip magazine	(2.9m)
Marca – daily football newspaper	(2.4m)
El País – daily newspaper	(2.1m)
Hola – weekly gossip magazine	(2m)
Diez Minutos – weekly magazine	(1.7m)
El Mundo – daily newspaper	(1.3m)
Lecturas – weekly gossip magazine	(1.1m)
As – daily football newspaper	(1m)
ABC – daily newspaper	(790,000)
El Periódico de Catalunya – daily newspaper	(790,000)

BANKING

Banking in Spain has improved almost beyond recognition over the last 15 years and in some aspects, e.g. cash machines, ranks among the most modern in the world. Opening a bank account is easy and can be done on the spot. Banks in resort areas have English-speaking staff and most banks cater for expatriate clients. The following are some of the main characteristics of Spanish banking.

- **Bank charges** – These are generally high and you can even be charged for paying money into your own account. Shop around and compare commissions, and if you carry out a lot of transactions other than cash deposits and withdrawals, ask your bank manager for a reduction on charges or a standard rate.

- **Bank managers** – Spanish bank managers are generally personable and approachable – many know most of their clients by name and work hard at keeping their business (which will come as a shock to most Britons).

- **Cash** – If you wish to withdraw cash using the services of a cashier, you need to show photographic identification as well as your bank card or book.

- **Cash machines** – Instructions are usually available in a number of languages including English. If you make a cash withdrawal from a machine that doesn't belong to your bank, there's a charge of between €2 and €4, depending on the amount you take out. Cash withdrawals made by credit card always attract commission – usually a percentage of the amount withdrawn.

> Spain is a cash society and withdrawals of large amounts (e.g. €3,000) are commonplace. If you need more than €4,000 in cash from your bank, you must order it at least a day in advance.

- **Cheques** – Payment by cheque is rare and few businesses or shops accept personal cheques. Beware of making out cheques to the bearer (*al portador*) as these can be cashed by anyone. You cannot stop payment by cheque once it has been made out unless it's lost or stolen, in which case you need to produce a police report (*denuncia*). The amount the lost or stolen cheque was made out for may not be 'refunded' to your account until six months afterwards.

- **Credit card payments** – Monthly credit card bills are usually paid by direct debit from your bank account. If you wish to make part payments, you must arrange this with your bank, not the credit card company.

Internet Security

Bogus emails claiming to be from your bank and asking for confidential information such as your account numbers and PIN are widespread in Spain. To avoid internet fraud, banks recommend you do the following:

- Never give personal or financial information by email to anyone (remember that banks never ask for confidential details by email).

- Never click on links included in emails claiming to be from your bank.

- Keep your anti-virus software regularly updated.

- Enter confidential information such as your user name, password and identity number only when using the bank's secure website.

- **Opening hours** – Opening hours are generally 8.30am to 1.30 or 2pm. Few banks remain open after 2pm and not all banks open on Saturdays (those that do open on Saturdays do so only from October to April).

- **Payment by debit & credit card** – For all payments made by card you need to show photographic identification. Spain has no chip and PIN system.

- **Queues** – Allow plenty of time for banking transactions, particularly if they involve cash. Although most banks now have single file queuing so that you wait for the first available desk or cashier, expect to queue for at least 20 minutes. To avoid queues, bank early in the morning or use cash machines.

- **Standing orders** – These are easy to set up and highly recommended – not least because it saves you time queuing at a bank. – but banks don't always pay them, so check your statements regularly.

TAXES

As you would expect in a country with millions of bureaucrats, the Spanish tax system is inordinately complicated and most Spaniards don't understand it. However, it's essential to be aware of which taxes you should be paying and when. Before you move to Spain, take expert advice, preferably from someone with knowledge of the tax systems in Spain and your home country, so that you can benefit from the advantages of tax planning.

Once in Spain, unless your Spanish is fluent enough to understand the paperwork, it's best to employ a financial advisor (*asesor fiscal*) for your tax matters.

> €500 notes are know in Spain as 'Bin Ladens', because when the single currency was introduced everyone knew they existed, but nobody had actually seen one.

The Spanish tax year is the calendar year and tax payments are usually made in arrears. Although Spain has a PAYE income tax system, for many other taxes the onus is on the taxpayer (i.e. you) to make payments and file returns.

Tax Fraud

Nowadays, it's difficult to avoid paying taxes in Spain and penalties are severe.

Nevertheless, tax evasion is still widespread – for decades, Spaniards have regarded avoiding taxes as an admirable feat rather than a crime. Payments in cash (therefore avoiding declaration of earnings and the payment of VAT) and under-declaring property prices are common, although large cash withdrawals (e.g. over €5,000) may be reported by the bank to the tax authorities if fraud is suspected.

Many foreigners, particularly retirees, the self-employed and those in casual employment, live and work in Spain without declaring their income to the tax authorities. This is illegal and you're liable to heavy fines. It's also difficult to prove that you're a resident (e.g. to avoid the non-resident retention when selling a property) if you haven't made any income tax declarations.

The tax authorities are permitted to claim unpaid taxes up to five years in arrears (plus interest) and you should keep all tax-related documentation for at least this long.

4.

BREAKING THE ICE

One of the best ways of getting over culture shock and feeling part of life in Spain is meeting and getting acquainted with Spaniards. Making new friends anywhere is never easy and the language and cultural barriers in Spain make it even harder. This chapter offers information on important aspects of Spanish society and the expatriate community, and advice on how to behave in social situations, topics to steer clear of in conversation, and dealing with confrontation.

> 'If there's one thing nearly everyone who lives and works abroad has to get right, it is this: they must be able to get along with the local people.'
>
> *Craig Storti, The Art of Crossing Cultures*

COMMUNITY LIFE

Spaniards like to live close to one another; their preference for apartment blocks is testimony to this. The vast majority of Spaniards live in apartments and in most cities and large towns it can be difficult to find any other type of accommodation.

Blocks tend to have at least four apartments per floor and many are high-rise and built around a central patio overlooked by kitchen windows, from which inhabitants hang out their washing. Walls and ceilings are often paper thin, particularly in blocks built during the '60s and '70s, and this, together with Spaniards' penchant for making noise, means that you can expect to hear your neighbours much of the time. Many Spaniards have no qualms about neighbours hearing their domestic goings-on (whether amorous or acrimonious) and television until the small hours. Summer evenings when windows are open and people go to bed later can be especially noisy.

Your neighbours are likely to be curious and want to know everything about you the minute you move in. If the block has a concierge (*portero*), he's usually the official broadcaster of news and you can rest assured that he will pass all information about you to other inhabitants. This curiosity is usually well intentioned and neighbours will probably offer you similar information about others in the block.

As soon as you move in, try to become part of your new

community. Introduce yourself to your neighbours and greet others in your block with a *buenos días* or *buenas tardes* whenever you meet in the lift or in the entrance. Use the communal facilities and, if possible, shop in local stores. This gives you the chance to practise your Spanish and others the opportunity to get to know you – receiving a greeting from neighbours or the baker makes you feel less alienated. However, the onus is on you to take the initiative, as few Spaniards will make an effort if you don't.

> One of Spain's top TV shows during 2005/6 was a sit-com – Aquí no hay quien viva – based on the goings-on of typical (i.e. nosy and discordant) inhabitants of an apartment block.

Community Regulations

Communities draw up regulations governing communal areas, e.g. patios, gardens, entrance halls and parking spaces, and private areas visible from outside such as balconies and facades. When you move into your accommodation, obtain a copy of the community rules and regulations, and read them carefully.

Community rules usually cover:

- noise levels;
- the keeping of pets – generally permitted, but not always;
- exterior decoration, e.g. colour of awnings and size of satellite dishes;
- rubbish disposal (where and when);
- the use of swimming pools and other recreational facilities;
- the hanging of laundry – in many communities this is prohibited on balconies.

Some communities impose few regulations, but others have long lists of rules owners must follow. Regulations are ratified by majority vote at community meetings and, although you may not agree with them, you're obliged to keep to them. If you wish to make a change to the exterior of your property or 'occupy' a communal area (e.g. to store a bicycle), request permission from the community first. If this isn't forthcoming, give up the idea rather than going against community regulations – it's better to be on neutral or good terms with your neighbours. Not only is it unpleasant to be on bad terms with those around you, but you never know when

you'll need to turn to a neighbour for help in a crisis or emergency.

SEXUAL ATTITUDES

At first glance, Spain appears to be a progressive and modern country with liberal attitudes to sex and marriage. This is one of the few countries in the Western world where homosexuals may marry (the union is called 'marriage' – *matrimonio*) and adopt children; politicians' and celebrities' extra-marital affairs aren't the subject of newspaper headlines and cause for public enquiry; all national newspapers carry explicit 'adult' adverts; and sex on television isn't confined to late-night viewing. Scratch the surface, however, and a strongly traditional society emerges in which men and women have clearly defined roles. This is particularly true in small towns and rural areas, where time-honoured Catholic values remain firmly in place. In your encounters with Spaniards of both sexes you can expect to experience both traditional and progressive attitudes.

Men

Spanish men's cultural make-up comprises two larger-than-life stereotypes: the Don Juan figure (derived from a character in Tirso de Molina's 17th-century play who seduces and then abandons women including a nun) and the Latin Lover, based on the reputation Spanish men earned for themselves during the '60s and early '70s, when foreign females were reportedly seduced in their thousands by slick, smooth-talking waiters in holiday resorts. Added to these is

the traditional Spanish view of the man as patriarch and defender of the family's honour.

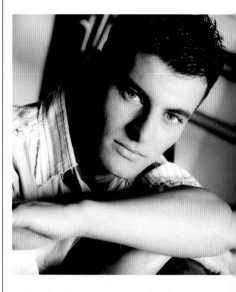

Despite the enormous gains in equality for women since 1980, *machismo* is still an intrinsic part of Spanish society. A recent survey by the Ministry of Social Affairs found that 70 per cent of men do no household chores and that nearly half of married women who work have sole responsibility for housework. It's still widely believed that a man who has several sexual

In 2004, 31,000 weddings in Spain (around 14 per cent of the total) had at least one foreign spouse: 44 per cent of these were between a Spanish man and foreign woman, 29 per cent between a Spanish woman and a foreign man, and the remainder between two foreigners.

partners is virile and a figure to be admired, whereas a woman in a similar situation is seen as 'easy' and may even be classed as a 'whore' by some more conservative sectors of society. These attitudes are found throughout Spain, although to a lesser extent in cities and coastal resorts where the influx of foreigners has led to a more cosmopolitan social outlook.

Spanish women often see foreign men as a breath of fresh air and may have high expectations of their views on equality, while foreign men may find Spanish women keen to show off their feminism and liberal views on sexual relationships. However, although many women (especially city-dwellers) are 'liberated', traditional values still

There's an active singles scene in cities but even here many single Spaniards complain that it's difficult to meet others. Internet dating is increasingly popular – a 2006 survey found that over 5m singles were registered on dating websites – and there are singles clubs in many cities and large towns.

prevail – so don't be surprised if what you considered to be a no-strings-attached relationship turns out to be much more serious and the woman has marriage high on her agenda. Although (Catholic) church weddings are decreasing, nearly two-thirds of marriages take place in church and if you marry a Spanish woman, you should expect a church wedding. Some people consider registry office marriages as invalid and even disgraceful.

Women

Foreign women have often been cast in the role of 'sex object', a vestige of the early days of package tourism, when Spanish beaches were invaded by scantily-clad foreign girls – to the delight of avid Spanish men anxious to show off their Latin Lover prowess. Times have changed, but there's still an undercurrent of this view and a foreign woman in Spain may find herself the object of unwelcome attention from men and disapproval from women. Expect male heads, particularly older ones, to turn (especially if you're blonde) and catcalls and remarks to come your way – these are usually harmless and meant as compliments, but it can be a humiliating experience.

A foreign woman in a relationship with a Spanish man inevitably comes up against the formidable figure of the mother-in-law (*suegra*), who usually has high hopes of her son marrying a chaste Spanish girl. There may be prejudice towards you because of your nationality – traditional Spaniards tend to have a particularly negative view of

Scandinavian and North American women, who are seen as 'wild' and 'loose' – and it may take a while for your future relatives to overcome this.

Abuse of Women

Sexual harassment in the workplace and violence at home are all too common in Spain, where one in ten working women suffers sexual harassment at work and an average of five women are murdered by their husbands or partners each month. The government has introduced legislation and measures designed to provide greater protection for women, but these have had little impact on the situation. Sexual harassment is particularly difficult to eradicate in Spanish society and there have been cases of women being dismissed after reporting sexual harassment in their workplace.

Homosexuals

Homosexual acts were prohibited under Franco but in recent years much has been done to create equality for homosexual couples, who now enjoy the same rights as heterosexuals. In 2005 Spain became one of the few countries in the world to allow homosexuals to marry, divorce and adopt children, though the measure, accepted by a large section of society, was strongly opposed by the Catholic church and the right-wing Partido Popular (PP). Nevertheless, while in the big cities many people are open-minded and homosexuality is tolerated and accepted – Madrid has a gay quarter (Chueca) and Gay Pride rallies are celebrated in Barcelona and Madrid every year – elsewhere Spaniards show little tolerance and few homosexuals come out of the closet.

MEETING PEOPLE

Many expats complain that it's difficult to establish friendships with Spaniards, who are friendly and welcoming but allow few foreigners to become more than acquaintances. Apart from the obvious cultural and language barriers, reasons for this are that Spaniards are very private people; they're very family-orientated and many of their friends come from their extended family; and many keep in contact with childhood and school friends. With a ready-established network of friends, most Spaniards see little need to seek friendship with foreigners.

You'll therefore usually need to make the first move when it comes to meeting Spaniards – and this is easier said than done, particularly if you're shy or unused to taking the initiative.

Meeting other expats is often easier and friendships may develop more naturally. Nevertheless, going out to meet local people is the first step to enjoying your time in Spain and lessening the effects of alienation and culture shock.

There are various ways of meeting Spaniards and other expats, including the following:

- **At work** – Meeting people isn't a problem if you're an employee, and among your colleagues may be several potential friends but you may have to take the initiative and ask others to join you for lunch or coffee. However, you shouldn't expect regular Friday evening drinks as is common in some countries. Office parties aren't common either, although many companies organise Christmas lunches and get-togethers for employees leaving their jobs. Social arrangements can be vague – someone may suggest going out on a Saturday night but make no specific arrangements. Foreigners are often disappointed or offended when nothing materialises, but this is normal and part of Spaniards' *mañana* attitude.

> Accept any social invitations that come your way (you can be choosy later) and don't forget to reciprocate.

- **Expatriate networks** – Most resort areas and large cities in Spain have expatriate networks whose activities encompass a range of clubs and social events. Look in the local expatriate press for details or contact your local embassy or consulate.

- **Language lessons** – These provide an ideal environment to meet other foreigners and, possibly, Spaniards learning English. Language schools and teachers usually organise regular social events. Setting up a language exchange (*intercambio*) often leads to new friends.

- **Local clubs** – Find out about clubs and societies in your area (town halls and local newspapers are good sources of information) and join one or two as soon as possible. If you play a sport, consider joining the local club – tennis leagues and golf competitions (not to mention the club house) are ideal for meeting people and keeping fit at the same time.

- **School or childcare facilities** – These provide plentiful opportunities for contact with other parents, especially when collecting children. Look on the school notice board for news about forthcoming events and meetings. Most schools have a parents' association (*asociación de padres y madres/APA* or *APMA*), which are worth joining and always welcome offers of help. Many *APA*s organise social events for parents as well as fundraising activities.

> Vegetarians are rare in Spain. If you're a vegetarian, don't expect your hosts to take this into account and be prepared for shocked faces and incredulity when (and if) you tell them.

Where & When to Meet

If you arrange to meet someone, choose a local bar or café. It's unusual to invite people to your home until you know them well, and you should never arrange to meet people at their home unless they suggest it. Be flexible about meeting times and remember that most Spaniards don't go out till at least 9pm.

Paying

If you arrange the get-together, you may be expected to pay. This is definitely the case if it's a business lunch or networking occasion, but at more informal gatherings, those present might take it in turns to pay for a round of drinks or *tapas* – make sure you pay for at least one round – or agree to share the bill. It's best not to be the one to suggest 'going Dutch' – a Spaniard may consider you stingy if you propose sharing the bill for a few drinks and *tapas*, which 'anyone' can afford. The Spanish are generous and often pay for others' drinks and *tapas* – make sure you reciprocate. If it's your birthday, tradition has it that you pay for drinks.

INVITATIONS

Receiving Invitations

Spaniards regard their home as a sanctuary – which is the main reason why so much of Spanish social life takes place outside – and if you receive an invitation to a Spaniard's home or a social occasion, consider yourself privileged. This indicates that your hosts have a high regard for you and constitutes a sign of friendship.

For a lunch invitation you should arrive around 2pm (although the meal may not be served until 3pm or later) and for dinner around 9pm, although your hosts will usually give you a time. It's rude to arrive earlier than the stated time and later than half an hour afterwards.

Invitations usually extend to your partner or spouse, but if your hosts aren't aware that you have a partner, it's acceptable to ask for him or her to be included. If you have children, you shouldn't bring them unless your hosts specifically invite them.

Dress Code

Your outfit will depend on the occasion and who else is going to be there. Older Spaniards dress up when receiving guests in their home but younger people tend to dress more casually. Don't be surprised, however, if other guests are dressed up – Spaniards take great pride in their appearance and most dress smartly even if the occasion is casual. If you don't know or haven't been told what sort of occasion it is, it's best to dress smartly. Men should

wear or take a jacket, but a tie isn't expected except on very formal occasions such as an engagement party. Avoid dressing too casually – jeans and trainers aren't usually acceptable.

Gifts

You may wish to take the hosts a gift as thanks for their hospitality. Usual gifts include a bottle of (good, Spanish) wine or a box of chocolates. A bouquet of flowers (not yellow or white or chrysanthemums of any colour – these symbolise death) is suitable for special occasions such as a birthday or anniversary.

The Meal

Most Spaniards serve two courses plus dessert at lunch and dinner, and there may be aperitifs before the meal. Portions for guests are usually generous and your hosts may insist on serving you extra – it's rude to decline as it looks as if you don't like the food.

You should keep your hands above the table at all times and use cutlery from the outside inwards, i.e. the cutlery on the extreme left and right is for the first course. Bread is usually served and you should break small pieces and eat them whole rather than bite into a large piece.

Drinks are usually offered on arrival. Most people start with beer, but beer is rarely served with the meal, which is normally accompanied by wine (invariably red) and water. Coffee or tea are never served with a meal, but you may be offered coffee afterwards

guests to come for lunch before 2pm or dinner before 9pm.

What to Serve

Serve drinks and 'nibbles' (e.g. olives and nuts) when guests arrive. Most guests will expect two courses plus dessert and large portions, so make sure you prepare more than sufficient – not having enough food to serve guests is high on the list of Spaniards' most embarrassing situations. Since homemade Spanish cooking is usually excellent, your guests may have high expectations of your cuisine. If you aren't a great cook, it's best to buy ready-made food (or not to host a meal at all). Avoid spicy recipes and unusual dishes unless you're preparing typical food from your country. You should provide salt and pepper, serviettes and plenty of bread.

Offer coffee after the meal (never during), but serve the coffee and milk separately, as many people prefer black coffee after food. You can offer tea, although you should expect few takers.

– expect strong, black coffee with a splash of milk served in a tiny cup. If you don't like *espresso*, decline politely but wait to be offered an alternative rather than asking – if your hosts haven't got what you ask for, they may feel offended.

Unless you know the hosts particularly well, stay seated while the meal is served and don't pour yourself wine or even water but wait for it to be offered. During or after the meal, don't clear anything away or offer to help – this will probably offend your hosts and few Spaniards allow outsiders to see their kitchen.

Making Invitations

If you invite Spaniards to your home for a meal, state clearly the occasion and the time – you should adapt this to the Spanish timetable and never expect

> Avoid phoning anyone at home between 2 and 5pm, when many Spaniards relax (and possibly sleep) after lunch, particularly in the summer. In the evening, it's best to phone before 10pm.

RESPECTING PRIVACY

Spaniards are essentially private people and keep themselves very much to themselves – they tend to rely on their close family for help with personal problems and rarely mention these to 'outsiders'. As a result, even if you've worked with someone for years you'll probably know very little about his life outside the workplace.

Although Spaniards are animated conversationalists and can talk for hours, topics of conversation with anyone other than family or close friends are usually of a neutral or general nature.

Loarre Castle, Aragon

Unless Spaniards offer personal information it's best not to ask, as you risk offending them deeply.

On the other hand, Spaniards have a seemingly insatiable appetite for details of other people's lives, and gossip magazines and TV programmes are devoured by millions. With this in mind, you might prefer not to provide too much information about your own life. In any case, some Spaniards find it embarrassing to be told personal details.

A Spaniard's home is a sanctum and you may never be invited to a friend's house. This isn't an affront but rather a reflection of the division between public and private life. Never press Spaniards for an invitation to their home and never appear unannounced on their doorstep.

TABOOS

Spaniards are generally relaxed and accommodating of foreigners' *faux pas*, but there are certain inexcusable social blunders and taboo subjects of conversation, which it's wise to be aware of. Below is a short guide to areas where you need to tread carefully.

Conversation

As in most countries, there are topics that should be avoided in conversation with Spaniards. These include:

> There are many older Spaniards who revere Franco and a surprising number of younger Spaniards who claim to feel nostalgia for his dictatorship – even though they weren't even born when it ended.

The Civil War

The Spanish Civil War (1936-39) split the country firmly into two camps and this deep division survives more than 60 years later. The vast majority of families were affected by the Civil War and almost everyone has an ancestor who was killed in the war or its aftermath or forced into exile.

The causes and effects of the war are rarely clear-cut for any Spaniard and few find it possible to be objective. Feelings still run high on the subject so, if possible, avoid stating an opinion about the Civil War and, if a Spaniard expresses an opinion you don't agree with, stay silent.

Franco

When compared to other recent dictatorships such as Pinochet's in Chile and the Military Junta in Greece, Franco's 40 years of absolute rule in Spain are surprisingly little discussed in Spain. The so-called 'pact of forgetting' (*pacto del olvido*) during the transition to democracy has meant that events of the period and their significance have been more or less brushed under the carpet. Only recently has Franco been referred to as a 'dictator' on television (previously he was referred to as a 'leader' or 'ruler') and only in the last few months have there been calls for a revision of history textbooks to give an impartial account of the dictatorship.

Spaniards are deeply divided not only over whether Franco's long dictatorship was good or bad for the country but even over whether Franco was a dictator – his supporters claim he was the only man capable of saving Spain and some refer to him as the 'father' of modern Spain.

Such attitudes are incomprehensible to many foreigners, particularly those coming from countries with long-established democracies, but given this situation, it's best to avoid any mention of Franco, say nothing if his name is mentioned and hope the subject is changed quickly.

Gibraltar

Almost all Spaniards claim that Gibraltar is Spanish and should be returned to Spain as soon as possible. Avoid bringing up the topic of Gibraltar (particularly if you're British) and comparing it to the Spanish enclaves of Ceuta and Melilla in Morocco – Spaniards are well armed with numerous arguments as to why the situation is **totally** different …

Religion

In spite of the fact that Spain is officially a secular state and that fewer than 50 per cent of Spaniards claim to be practising Catholics, Spain is very much a Catholic country and (Catholic) religion plays an important part in society.

The vast majority of Spaniards have been christened and had their first communion in the Catholic faith, most have (Catholic) church weddings and baptise their children in the Catholic faith. It's therefore best to avoid expressing negative

opinions about religion, the Catholic church or the Pope.

Spain & Spanish Customs

Spaniards are fiercely proud of their country and its way of life, and generally find it hard to take criticism, particularly from foreigners. When you're with Spaniards, avoid negative comments about Spain and Spanish customs – keep these thoughts to yourself or share them only with other expats – and don't join in a conversation between Spaniards about Spain unless you have something good to say.

Dress

On the whole, Spaniards dress smartly when on public view, even if it's just to pop to the shops. At home, many wear casual or 'working' clothes (e.g. a housecoat or tracksuit), but it's common practice to change before you leave the house.

Bare body parts are frowned on and most Spaniards consider it rude for women to be in a public place wearing a bikini, men bare-chested or anyone barefoot – many establishments such as supermarkets, shopping centres and restaurants refuse entry to men without at least a T-shirt and anyone without shoes. It's considered offensive to sit down to a meal in a swimsuit or without a top on. The Spanish consider that beach and swimwear is for the beach, pool and garden only.

EXPATRIATE COMMUNITY

Over 8 per cent of the Spanish population are foreigners and just about every nationality is represented.

Few parts of Spain are now without an immigrant population, although 60 per cent of foreigners are concentrated on the coasts and islands. Some neighbourhoods such as Lavapiés in Madrid and Ciutat Vella in Barcelona are melting pots of foreign cultures and many resort areas such as Benalmadena on the Costa del Sol and Altea on the Costa Blanca have foreign populations that outnumber the locals.

In 2006 Spain's foreign population numbered 3.73m, a figure expected to rise to 6.5m by 2010.

If you move to an area that's popular with other people of your nationality, the lack of cultural and language barriers makes socialising much easier. Many resort areas and large cities have well established expat networks, and fitting into these is often straightforward. But you should beware of becoming too dependent on expatriate society, which can be unstable (expats tend to come and go) and claustrophobic, particularly in small communities where little goes on and everyone knows everything about everyone else. Try to extend your contacts further afield and make an effort to meet the locals too – getting to know Spaniards will add variety and interest to your social life, and open new doors to you.

Advantages

- It's easier to fit in with people of your own nationality.
- You get the chance to relax and speak your own language.
- It's a means of letting off steam after the stress of culture shock.

Disadvantages

- Spending too much time with expats may mean you don't accept your move as definitive.
- Time spent with other expats could be spent fitting into life with Spaniards.

- Many expatriate groups are little more than an excuse to complain about everything Spanish – this may accentuate your own negative feelings towards Spain and doesn't help you settle in.
- Expat groups tend to be a varied bunch of people, perhaps not necessarily those you would mix with in your home country – you're drawn together by circumstances more than by genuine interest – and you may find yourself socialising with people you don't like.

CONFRONTATION

Spaniards are generally hot-blooded and have quick tempers but they usually avoid confrontation. If a Spaniard doesn't agree with something, his way of showing this may be to stay silent, which can be confusing for foreigners – particularly Americans, who are more used to active disagreement.

To many Spaniards, it's impolite to disagree with someone in front

> If you're stopped by the police for any reason – they may simply wish to check your identity documentation – be polite and use *usted*. There's little point in being obstructive or arguing, which may in fact make things worse for you. If you think you've been stopped or fined illegally, make a complaint at a police station afterwards.

of others, particularly in a situation such as the workplace, where there are superiors present. Staying silent is also a practical tactic since disagreements can quickly turn into loud and unpleasant shouting matches.

As far as possible, it's best to remain calm and avoid confrontation with Spaniards – little (or nothing) is achieved by it and you may earn yourself the unwelcome reputation as a difficult foreigner.

When Spaniards get angry, it rarely lasts long and most are quick to make amends – harbouring ill feelings towards other people is discouraged. Children involved in arguments are encouraged to make up almost immediately by apologising and shaking hands.

DEALING WITH OFFICIALS

Given the bureaucratic nature of Spanish society, you're likely to have frequent encounters with officials, e.g. civil servants, the police and notaries. Officials in Spain are commonly perceived as superior to the average Spaniard.

There are numerous historical reasons for this, not least Spain's 40 years of dictatorship, when officials in uniform, particularly the police, represented the repressive state and were to be feared. Traditionally, anyone in uniform (even a ticket collector at a theatre) was awarded a certain respect and consequently acted as a superior human being. Nowadays, this deference isn't so marked, but there are nevertheless certain codes of behaviour you should follow when dealing with officials (see below).

Golden Rules for Dealing with Officials

- Always use the *usted* form of address.
- Always be polite.
- Always stay calm and never lose your temper.
- Dress smartly – this earns you respect.
- Don't expect officials to smile – many have an innate ability to remain poker-faced in any situation.

Police

Under Franco, the police had enormous power and were used to repress any resistance, often violently – many Spaniards recall the police's brutal repression of protestors during the '70s and cases of torture by police during the dictatorship. Since the advent of democracy, the role of Spain's three police forces has been limited to maintaining law and order, and rarely do they abuse their authority, but for many people they still represent state repression and are to be feared.

> In 2005, the number of UK nationals resident in Spain rose by 30 per cent and accounted for 6.1 per cent of the foreign population, mainly concentrated in the provinces of Alicante and Malaga.

Civil Servants

Spanish civil servants hold the key to many essential permissions, such as your residence (and work) permit, social security card and driving licence, and your encounters with them are likely to be frequent. In your dealings with civil servants be as polite and calm as possible and always thank them for their help.

Few civil servants speak English and you shouldn't expect them to – take an interpreter if your Spanish is poor. Some town councils, particularly those in resort areas, and some utility companies have English-speaking staff but they aren't always available – find out when their shifts are and go then, but don't expect them to speak fluent English. Speak slowly and carefully, and be prepared to repeat things several times.

Remember that they're doing you a favour by speaking English.

Teachers

All teachers in the Spanish state school system are civil servants and their jobs are clearly defined and regulated. Few arrive early or leave late and all school business, with the exception of staff meetings, takes place within school hours. Therefore, don't expect a teacher to stay behind after school to see you or help your child with his work – some teachers do so if asked, but most will see parents and children only during school hours. If you wish to see the head teacher, you should phone first for an appointment.

All classes are conducted in Spanish (except foreign languages), all correspondence from schools is in Spanish and few teachers speak English. In your dealings with a school and teachers, it's polite to ask first if someone speaks English rather than starting a conversation in English; if your Spanish isn't good enough, take an interpreter along with you.

Casares, Andalucia

5.

THE LANGUAGE BARRIER

Being able to communicate with Spaniards and knowing what to do and say when you meet them are priorities when you move to Spain, especially when you first arrive. Learning to speak a foreign language is never easy and full of potential pitfalls – all expats have stories to tell of when they said 'the wrong thing', often with embarrassing consequences. To help keep your own collection of anecdotes as small as possible, this chapter offers tips on learning Spanish and regional languages and explanations of body and sign language (and their importance in communication), false friends, forms of address and greetings, and telephone and letter etiquette.

In several parts of Spain, particularly the popular *Costas* and Tenerife, English is widely spoken and in some areas – such as Arroyo de la Miel in Benalmádena (Costa del Sol), Playa de las Américas (Tenerife) and Torreblanca (Costa Blanca) – you may wonder if you're in Spain at all. In others, however, little or no English is spoken and if you want to make any progress with your life you must speak Spanish. Wherever you are in Spain, unless you learn Spanish, there's a strong tendency to rely heavily on other expats for your needs. This can be expensive and even dangerous – Spain, particularly the *Costas*, is full of expat 'experts' waiting to prey on their compatriots and relieve them of their money.

> 'Language is the source of misunderstandings.'
>
> Antoine de Saint-Exupéry (French writer)

LEARNING SPANISH

Relocation and culture shock experts generally agree that one of the best ways of settling into a foreign country where your language isn't spoken is to learn the local language as soon as possible. Even a basic knowledge of a few key phrases when you arrive will help you feel more in control (or less out of control) in everyday situations.

Expatriates with no language knowledge tend to feel vulnerable since all they can do is nod and gesture – some people also feel a strong sense of ridicule when they have no tools of verbal expression.

The benefits of mastering the basics are enormous and it will do wonders to boost your self-esteem and sense of achievement when you first set foot in Spain. What most foreigners refer to as Spanish is actually Castilian (*castellano*), the only language spoken throughout Spain and understood by the vast majority of Spaniards. All references to Spanish throughout this book are to Castilian, spoken by 65 per cent of Spaniards as their first and only language. The other 35 per cent speak Spanish and a regional language.

The Spanish Alphabet

The Spanish alphabet has 29 letters: a to z (as in English) plus ch, ll and ñ. All accents are acute and placed only on vowels, e.g. é and í. The 'u' occasionally carries a dieresis – ü, e.g. pingüino

---

Why Spanish is Essential

- In an accident or emergency, knowing what to say in Spanish could save your (or someone else's) life.

- Your chance of finding a job or making a success of being self-employed increases dramatically.

- You save time and money on translations and don't have to rely on others to help you.

- Culture shock and the sense of being a stranger in Spain diminish.

- Locals will appreciate your efforts and this will help you fit in more easily.

- Spanish culture is easier to appreciate if you speak some Spanish.

- Your circle of friends will be widened beyond other English-speaking expatriates.

- It opens doors that are often closed to non-Spanish speakers, particularly in less cosmopolitan parts of Spain.

- Joining a language class is an excellent way of meeting people

Know Before You Go

To give yourself the best chance, start learning Spanish well in advance of your departure – at least six months if possible. Don't believe anyone who claims that the best way to learn a language is to go to the country and 'immerse yourself' in it. While this is a good way of improving existing knowledge, experts generally agree that this is the worst way to learn a language from scratch – not only are you under stress from the logistics of your recent relocation, but you're also prone to picking up errors in the language, which are difficult to correct later. It's far better to gain a grounding in the basics before you leave; knowing how to ask for things and understanding something of what is being said will make settling in easier.

To give yourself the best possible chance when you arrive in Spain make your language learning as intensive as possible. Specialist language schools are available in many large cities and the Cervantes Institute (the official Spanish cultural representative abroad) offers language classes and opportunities to experience Spanish culture in nearly 40 countries around the world (UK offices are in Leeds, London and Manchester – ⌨ www.cervantes.es).

A list of words and phrases you might need during your first few days in Spain can be found in **Appendix A**.

Once in Spain

When you arrive in Spain make sure you commit yourself to some sort of learning method as soon as possible, preferably within the first week, rather than merely hoping that you'll 'pick it up as you go along'. There are literally thousands of language schools throughout the country with Spanish courses (*español para extranjeros*) to suit all levels and budgets. Cheaper courses are offered to residents by local councils in many areas; courses are subsidised and are held at branches of the Official Language School (Escuela Oficial de Idiomas/EOI), particularly those located in resort areas (EOI, C/ Jesús Maestro s/n, 28003 Madrid,

☎ 915 335 802, ⌨ www.eoidiomas. com). Shop around to compare tuition fees and teaching methods, and if the course is expensive ask whether you can have a free trial lesson before you commit yourself.

Private teachers are readily available. Advantages include individual attention and tailored learning, which should lead to faster progress, but private tuition is considerably more expensive (expect to pay at least €20 per hour, more in large cities). A cheap alternative (or supplement) to language classes is a 'language exchange' (*intercambio*) with someone keen to practise his English (or your native tongue). Arrange to meet on a regular basis and spend half the time speaking English (or another foreign language) and half speaking Spanish. This is also a good way to make friends. You can advertise for a private teacher or language exchange in local newspapers, on bulletin and notice boards (in shopping centres, supermarkets, universities, clubs, etc.), and through your or your partner's employers.

> Spanish is the world's third most widely spoken language (after Mandarin and Hindi) and over 380m people's mother tongue.

Tips for Learning Spanish

- **Stay motivated** – Take every opportunity that comes your way to practise, even if it's just asking a waiter the time.

- **Persevere** – Practice makes perfect and even if you make a mess of your carefully prepared sentence, Spaniards are usually patient and forgiving of mistakes made by foreigners.

- **Practise your 'rr'** whenever you can (and you're alone) – roll that tongue while sitting in traffic jams and instead of singing in the shower.

> All children should learn to say their telephone number and address in Spanish as soon as possible.

- **Don't set yourself impossible targets** – Expect to learn gradually and be prepared for the 'plateau' at intermediate level, where you've learnt the basics but seem to make no progress for weeks.

Muy importante!

- **Don't obsess yourself with the subjunctive** – a difficult concept for a native English-speaker to grasp. Try to learn the basics of it, but if you don't use it or use it wrongly people will still understand you.

- **Learn at least ten new words a week.**

- **Laugh at your own mistakes.**

- **Take pride in your progress** – Pat yourself on the back when you manage to communicate something successfully.

Children

If you're relocating as a family to Spain, your children also need to learn Spanish. For most children, studying in Spanish isn't such a handicap as it may at first appear, particularly for those aged below ten. The majority of children adapt quickly to a new language and most become reasonably fluent within three to six months. However, not all children adapt equally well to a change of language and culture, particularly children over ten, many of whom have great difficulties during their first year. Children who are already bilingual (in two other languages) usually have little problem learning Spanish, while monolingual children tend to find it more difficult. Spanish children are generally friendly towards foreign children, who often acquire a 'celebrity status' (particularly in rural schools), which helps their integration.

Before you leave, set up language classes for your children and ensure they learn the basics.

> Spain is also home to the following minority languages:
>
> Aranés – spoken by around 7,000 people in the small Vall d'Aran in the Catalan Pyrenees (in the province of Lleida); Bable – this ancient tongue is spoke by around 100,000 Spaniards in the north of León province and Asturias and is experiencing a revival.

This is especially important if you plan to send your children to a Spanish school – just being able to say '*Hola, me llamo Megan*' and count up to a hundred does wonders for your child's confidence on that difficult first day. Once you've arrived, keep up language classes outside school until your children can fend for themselves. Children in a Spanish school will need extra lessons initially to help them settle into their class and make friends.

Foreign children are tested and put into a class suited to their level of Spanish, even if this means being taught with younger children.

Children who don't read and write Spanish are often set back a year to compensate for their lack of Spanish and different academic background.

Once a child has acquired a sufficient knowledge of spoken and written Spanish, he's assigned to a class appropriate to his age. Some state schools provide intensive Spanish lessons ('bridging classes') for foreign children, although this is by no means the norm. It may be worthwhile enquiring about the availability of extra Spanish classes before choosing where to live.

If your local school doesn't provide extra Spanish classes, your only choice will be to pay for private lessons or send your children to another (possibly private) school, where extra Spanish tuition is provided. Some parents send children to an English-speaking school for a year before enrolling them in a bilingual or Spanish school, while other parents believe it's better to throw their children in at the deep end than to introduce them gradually to the language. It all depends on the character, ability and wishes of the child. Whatever you decide, it will help your children **enormously** if they have intensive Spanish lessons before arriving in Spain.

OTHER LANGUAGES

Spain has three official regional languages: Basque (*euskera*), Catalan (*catalán*) and Galician (*gallego*), which have equal status with Spanish in the regions where they're spoken. Road signs, street and building names, notices and official documents are usually in the regional language rather than Spanish, causing considerable problems for foreigners who know only Spanish and even for Spaniards from other regions.

> If your move to a bi-lingual area is for less than two years, learn some basic phrases in the regional language (as well as Spanish) to help you fit into local society. If your move is longer term, it's a good idea to learn the regional language as well as Spanish.

This is an important consideration if you plan to relocate to the Basque Country, Catalonia, the Balearics, Galicia or Valencia. In these regions, communications from the authorities may be in the local language only and many officials are reluctant to speak any other language. In some areas, it may be difficult to settle in if you don't speak the regional language. You may find that bi-lingual Spaniards will happily chat to you in Spanish but slip into their regional language when talking to each other. Don't be offended by this, as they aren't excluding you but merely doing what comes naturally to them. It's also worth bearing in mind that many bi-lingual Spaniards are fiercely proud of their regional language and defend its use ardently – never underestimate Nationalist feelings (which often run very high) and never scorn a regional language.

> Catalán is the seventh most widely spoken European language.

Catalan

Catalan is the most widely-spoken of Spain's three official regional languages and some 6.5m people in Catalonia, the Balearics and Valencia, including the Costa del Azahar and Costa Blanca (as well as Andorra and parts of south-west France). Catalan has several dialects, e.g. *Mallorquín* (spoken on Majorca), *Menorquín* (spoken on Minorca) and *Valenciano* (spoken in Valencia). The degree to which Catalan is spoken varies with the area: in some places Spanish is more widely spoken than Catalan – e.g. in Barcelona, where less than half the population speaks fluent Catalan – and the southern Costa Blanca, where *Valenciano* is hardly heard at all (although state schools teach almost all subjects in *Valenciano*); in others, Catalan dominates speech and some people rarely speak anything else or may even refuse to.

Galician

Some 2.5m people in Galicia speak Galician and a surprising number (mostly in rural areas) don't speak any Spanish. If you plan to move to an urban area in Galicia, it probably won't be necessary to learn Galician, but if your chosen spot is a village, it may be essential if you wish to have any contact with your neighbours.

Basque

Basque is the least widely-spoken of Spain's regional languages and by far the most difficult – it's cluttered with consonants and unfathomable by anyone who hasn't learned it (at least with Catalan and Galician, Spanish speakers can get an idea of what's being said). Although Basque has enjoyed a revival over the last few years, it's mainly spoken in rural areas and few Basques don't speak Spanish, so it isn't essential to learn it.

Education in Bi-lingual Regions

Most state and private schools in areas where a regional language is spoken teach the vast majority of subjects in the regional language, e.g. in Catalonia all subjects (except Spanish and foreign languages) are taught in Catalan. This means that your children have the challenge of learning the regional language as well as Spanish.

If you feel this would be beyond their capabilities, it's best to send them to an international school, where subjects are usually taught in English.

Caló is a dialect spoken by many of Spain's 650,000 gypsies.

Dialects & Accents

Like most languages, Spanish is spoken with an infinite number of accents, which vary from one region and province to another and often even within a province. It's generally accepted that the easiest accent to understand is that of central Spain, i.e. in and around Madrid and the two Castiles, where Spaniards have the reputation of speaking clearly, or 'listening to themselves as they speak'.

Basque flag

Andalusian accents are among the most difficult to understand – 'c's are often pronounced as 's's and plural endings not pronounced at all; in some rural areas, even native speakers find comprehension a challenge. It can be a shock to a foreigner with a reasonable level of Spanish to discover that he cannot understand a word of what he hears. However, perseverance pays off and it doesn't take long to 'tune into' a regional accent and understand the essentials of what is being said.

There are also regional and local variations in vocabulary and grammar – i.e. different dialects. For example, 'small' is '*pequeño*' in standard Spanish, but '*chico*' is used throughout Andalusia. '*Autobús*' is the accepted word for a bus in mainland Spain, but in the Canaries it's a '*guagua*'.

SLANG & SWEARING

Like all languages, Spanish has a rich vocabulary of slang and swear words, the use of which depends on the company and the context.

Unless your Spanish is proficient, however, it's best to avoid using either – it's usually the case that only native speakers know when it's appropriate to which expression. All too often foreigners make terrible *faux pas* by swearing inappropriately or using slang in the wrong context. It's important to understand slang and swear words, however, and a useful guide is *Pardon My Spanish!* (Harraps).

BODY & SIGN LANGUAGE

Watch a group of Spaniards talking on the street and you may be amazed at the number of times they move their arms, hands and sometimes bodies as well during a conversation

– the Spanish are very expressive and gesticulation forms an essential part of conveying your message.

To an outsider (particularly the more reserved British), Spaniards' gesticulating may appear aggressive. However, most foreigners find themselves doing it too after a while.

Gestures

You may come across the following typically Spanish gestures. It isn't wise to imitate them until you're proficient in Spanish or it may be thought that you're mocking.

- **Rubbing thumb and forefinger together** – Something is very expensive or someone is very rich.
- **Running your index and middle fingers down the sides of your nose** – You're broke.
- **Holding both hands upwards while opening and shutting your fingers** – A place is crowded.
- **Lightly slapping your cheek with one hand** – Someone has a cheek (i.e. is impertinent).
- **Shaking your hand up and down in front of you** – You're amazed or disbelieving.

Personal Space

In a country with such a low population density you might expect the Spanish to want to spread out, but in spite of all the unoccupied countryside Spaniards like to live crowded together in flats, apparently don't object to paper-thin walls in apartment blocks and are quite happy to sit towel-to-towel on the beach.

Spaniards also like to move in

close to their conversation partners, keep tight up to the person in front of them in a queue and don't seem to mind elbowing their way through crowds.

> If a Spaniard puts two fingers up in a V-sign, don't be offended: he just means two. A V-sign with the palm facing outwards means victory. As in many other countries, it's offensive to raise your middle finger.

If you feel that your personal space has been encroached upon or even threatened by this closeness, don't take offence and try not to react as if you've been insulted – take a discreet step backwards or, if your personal space is vitally important, move to rural Spain.

FALSE FRIENDS

Some words in Spanish are similar in appearance to English words but have a different meaning, which can lead to misunderstanding and, in a few cases, embarrassment.

These words are often known as 'false friends'. The following is a brief guide to the false friends you're most likely to come across in everyday situations, with examples of the correct use of the Spanish words.

- *actualmente*: currently or at the moment, e.g. *Actualmente estoy en paro*. (I'm currently unemployed)
  actually: *de hecho*, e.g. *De hecho, no tengo ni idea*. (Actually, I don't have a clue.)
- *agenda*: diary
  agenda: *orden del día*
- *asistir*: to attend, go to, e.g. *Asistí a su boda*. (I attended his wedding.)
  assist: *ayudar*
- *atender*: to pay attention, e.g. *¿Estáis atendiendo al profesor?* (Are you paying attention to the teacher?) attend: *asistir* or *ir a*
- *ático*: top floor flat (highly sought-after and very expensive)
  attic: *desván*
- *carpeta*: file or folder
  carpet: *alfombra* or *moqueta*
- *compromiso*: obligation or commitment, e.g. *Tengo un compromiso ineludible este fin de semana*. (I have a commitment I can't get out of this weekend.)
  compromise: *acuerdo*
- *constipado*: to have a cold, e.g. *Estoy muy constipado*. (I've got a terrible cold.)
  constipated: *estreñido*

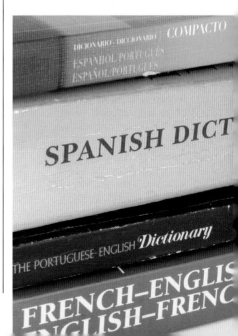

● *decepción*: disappointment, e.g. *Qué decepción – no puede venir.* (It's disappointing she can't come.)
deception: *engaño*

> When a Spaniard enters a waiting room, bank, café or shop, he often greets those present with a 'buenos días' or 'buenas tardes', irrespective of the number of people there or whether he knows anyone. It's polite to reply with a similar greeting.
>
> When they enter a restaurant or come across someone eating, many Spaniards say 'Qué aproveche' ('Enjoy your meal'). The correct reply is 'Gracias'.

● *embarazada*: pregnant, e.g. *María está embarazada.* (María is pregnant.)
embarrassing: *vergonzoso* or *vergüenza*, e.g. *¡Qué vergüenza.* (How embarrassing.)

● *gracioso*: funny, witty, e.g. *El actor es muy gracioso.* (The actor is very funny.)
gracious: *elegante* or *con gracia*

● *ignorar*: to be unaware of, e.g. *Ignoro su paradero.* (I'm unaware of his whereabouts.)
ignore: *no hacer caso*, e.g. *No me hizo caso.* (He ignored me.)

● *invitar*: to invite (and offer to pay), e.g. *Te invito a comer.* (I'll treat you to lunch.)

● *librería*: bookshop,
library: *biblioteca*

● *preciso*: necessary, e.g. *Es preciso aprender bien los verbos.* (It's necessary to/you must learn the verbs properly.)
precise: *exacto*

● *preservativo*: condom,
preservative: *conservante*

● *pretender*: to have the intention of doing something, e.g. *Pretende ser gracioso.* (He's trying to be funny.)
pretend: *fingir* or *simular*, e.g. *Finge que duerme.* (He's pretending to be asleep.)

● *sensible*: sensitive, e.g. *Llora fácilmente porque es muy sensible.* (He's cries easily because he's very sensitive.)
sensible: *sensato*, e.g. *Es una niña sensata.* (She's a sensible girl.)

● *simpático*: nice, friendly, e.g. *Los españoles son simpáticos.* (Spaniards are friendly.)
sympathetic: *comprensivo*

● *sport*: casual (as in clothing), e.g. *No se suele vestir de sport para el trabajo.* (People don't usually dress casually for work.)
sport: *deporte*

● *tópico*: cliché, e.g. *Es un tópico que todos los andaluces cantan flamenco.* (It's a cliché that all Andalusians can sing flamenco.)
topic: *tema* or *asunto*

There are several words in Spanish where a change in a vowel sound can cause red faces, e.g.:

- *Cojines* are cushions, *cajones* are drawers, but *cojones* is slang for testicles.
- *Pollo* is chicken, but *polla* is slang for penis (so be careful what you ask the butcher for).

> In 2005 the most popular names were Alejandro and Daniel for boys and Lucía and María for girls.

FORMS OF ADDRESS

Tú or *Usted?*

In common with many other European languages (but not English), Spanish makes a clear and important distinction between the formal or polite (*usted/Vd*) and informal or familiar (*tú*) modes of address, similar to *tu* and *vous* in French, and *du* and *Sie* in German.

As English has only one word for you, native English-speakers often find it difficult to decide when to use *usted* and *tú*. The decision is important, because if you address someone as *tú* when you should have used *usted*, you may offend him or it may be taken as a sign of disrespect, although most Spaniards make allowances for foreigners.

As a general rule, *usted* should be used whenever you address adults you don't know well, particularly older people, and *tú* should be used for friends and young people, including children. When socialising, however, you can use *tú* with people of your own age, even if meeting them for the first time.

There are some grey areas and the use of *tú* when you first meet someone is increasingly common, particularly among younger Spaniards. Nevertheless, it's best to err on the side of caution and, when in doubt, use *usted*. Once you've met someone a few times or have spent a while in his company, he will probably suggest that you use the *tú* form (*tutearse*). Note that in the Canaries (and much of South America), the informal form of address is rarely used except between children – even children address their parents as *usted*.

The plural of *tú* is *vosotros* and the plural of *usted* is *ustedes*.

Surnames & Titles

Spaniards have two surnames or family names (*apellidos* – the first is the father's first surname and the second the mother's first surname) and a wife keeps her maiden surnames on marriage, which can lead to confusion over what to call who when. For example, if José Gómez Pérez and Ana Sánchez Jiménez marry, they're addressed jointly as (*los*) *Señores de Gómez Pérez*, but when the wife is alone she is addressed as *Señora Sánchez Jiménez*. Their children, María and Alberto, are called *María*

Gómez Sánchez and *Alberto Gómez Sánchez*.

The use of the second surname is often dropped when referring to someone and many Spaniards introduce themselves with just their first surname. However, all official documentation, identity cards and many forms require two surnames (*apellido 1*, *apellido 2*).

You should address older people as *Señor* or *Señora*, or *Don* (male) or *Doña* (female). If you don't know a person's name, say simply *Señor* or *Señora*. If you're on familiar terms with people, address them simply by their first name.

Children

When addressing children (and even young adults, depending on your age) you should always use the *tú* form.

If you relocate to Spain with children, make sure they practise the *usted* form of address, which they will need for most situations in which they're addressing adults (the *tú* form is usually acceptable when addressing friends' parents).

GREETINGS

When you're introduced to a Spaniard you should shake hands and say '*encantado*' (if you're a man), '*encantada*' (if you're a woman) or '*mucho gusto*' ('nice to meet you'); you should do the same at the end of the meeting. Female acquaintances kiss each other, as do a man and a woman who know each other, usually on both cheeks (on one cheek in the Canaries), although the kiss is more of a brush on the cheek than an actual kiss.

Male friends sometimes use a two-hand shake where the right hand shakes the other's hand and the left hand is placed on the other's right forearm near the wrist. Male relatives and close friends embrace. With children the form of greeting is usually two kisses (one in the Canaries) for children up to the age of around 12. Older girls expect to be greeted with two kisses, but older boys expect to shake hands.

Informal greetings are '*hola*' ('hello' or 'hi') or '*buenas*' (an informal 'good day'), which should obviously be used only with children or people you know well. Otherwise, you should use '*buenos días*' ('good morning') until midday (around 1pm), '*buenas tardes*' ('good afternoon') from lunchtime until around 9 or 10pm, and '*buenas noches*' after that. '*Adiós*' is 'goodbye', although the more informal '*hasta luego*' ('see you later') or '*hasta pronto*' ('see you soon') are more frequently used. There's no need to add *Señor(a)* to greetings, even in a formal setting.

Teach your children both informal and formal greetings.

TELEPHONE, LETTERS & EMAIL

The use of email is becoming increasingly common in Spain but the telephone is still the preferred means of communication for the vast majority of people, both in a businesses context and for private communication. Letters are often used, particularly in businesses, although given the slowness and unreliability of the Spanish postal service, many are sent by fax rather than post.

Telephone

As in many other countries, telephone communication is increasingly by mobile (around 33m mobiles operate in Spain). When you answer the telephone, whether formally or informally, you should say '*Diga*' or '*Dígame*' ('Speak' or 'Speak to me'). Some people answer with '*¿Quién es?*' (literally, 'Who is it?') or a plain '*¿Sí?*', although this can be regarded as rude. Businesses often say the name of the company followed by a greeting such as '*Buenos días*' or '*¿En qué puedo ayudarle?*' ('How can I help you?'). As a general rule, always use *usted* when speaking to someone you don't know on the telephone unless it's obviously a child.

Letters

Starting

Formal letters start with '*Estimado señor/ Muy señor mío*' (for a male addressee) or '*Estimada señora/ Muy señora mía*' (for a female addressee). If you know the name of the person you're addressing a letter to, the opening should include it, e.g. '*Estimado Sr Lima*'. Informal letters start with '*Querido/Querida*' ('Dear') plus the addressee's name, e.g. '*Querido Pedro*'. As a general rule, if you normally address the person you're writing to as *usted*, you should use the formal beginning (and sign-off – see below).

Addresses

Addresses are usually written as follows:

Name of recipient:
Sr Don José Gómez,
Street name and number:
C/ Mayor, 24
Post code and town or city:
29640 Fuengirola
Province:
Málaga

Date

Dates are usually written in full and often include the day of the week, e.g. *martes, 10 de octubre de 2006*. You may also come across the numerical form, e.g. *10/6/06*. If the date is written directly above or below the signature, it may be preceded by the name of the place where the letter is signed, e.g. *En Marbella, a 10 de octubre de 2006*. This is particularly common on official documents, tax forms and cheques.

Signing off

There are several options for ending a formal letter (listed in order of formality):

- *Atentamente* (the equivalent of 'Yours faithfully' or 'Yours sincerely');

- *Sin otro particular, reciba un cordial saludo* or simply *Reciba un cordial saludo* (the equivalent of 'With regards') – *Recibe un cordial saludo* when you use the *tú* form of address;

Informal letters are usually ended with one of the following (in order of formality):

- *Un abrazo* (literally, 'a hug');
- *Un beso* or *Besos* (literally, 'a kiss'/'kisses' and the equivalent of 'With love').

Email

Email culture is gradually creeping into Spanish society, although a surprising number of businesses and professionals have no email address. If you're sending an email to someone you don't know, use formal address and language – the easy-going emails starting with a 'Hi' and first name terms that are prevalent in other countries, e.g. the UK, aren't common in Spain and Spaniards may be offended at your use of their first name when they haven't met you.

Most official organisations and large companies have email addresses, but many are notoriously bad at replying so don't be surprised if your email goes unanswered. If you need an urgent reply it's best to telephone.

Avila city walls, Castile y León

Guggenheim museum, Bilbao

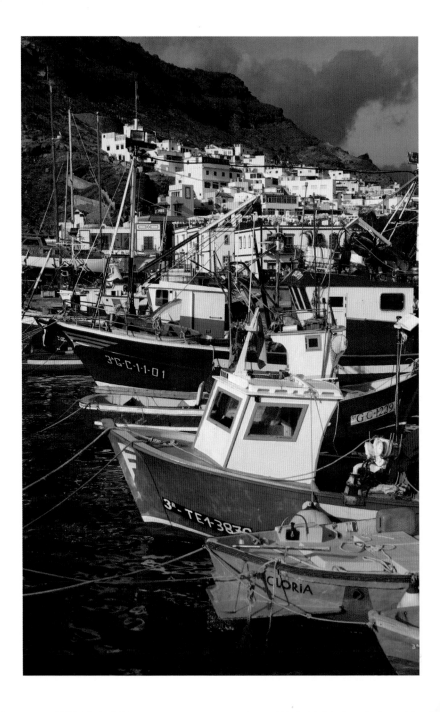

6.

THE SPANISH AT WORK

One of the most common mistakes foreigners make when coming to Spain to work or start a business is to assume that they can continue working in the way they did in their home country, particularly if they had a successful business there. Many expatriates completely underestimate the dramatic differences in business culture between the Spanish and northern Europeans and Americans, for example. Working in Spain usually involves a fairly steep learning curve for a foreigner – professionally, linguistically and culturally.

This chapter provides information on working for or with the Spanish, setting up a business and business etiquette.

> The Spanish word for retirement is 'jubiliación' – literally 'jubilation'.

WORK ETHIC

Spaniards work to live rather than live to work, and a job is viewed mainly as a means of earning money to spend in your leisure time rather than a way of fulfilling ambition or talent. This doesn't mean that the Spanish aren't hard workers, but they don't believe a person is better for working harder and longer, and cannot understand why employees in some other countries are prepared to forgo their family, holidays and free time in favour of their job.

PERMITS & PAPERWORK

As you would perhaps expect, the pernicious red tape for which Spain is notorious rears its ugly head highest when it comes to working in Spain, particularly if you're a non-EU citizen and/or plan to set up a business. Setting up a business is fraught with bureaucratic obstacles for the Spanish let alone foreigners, and the process can take several months, if not over a year. Obtaining a work permit (non-EU citizens only) is also extremely difficult and obstructions in your way include employment quotas that are rarely relaxed and preference given to EU citizens for any job vacancy.

The maxim 'patience is a virtue' is never more true than if you're in either of the above situations. But the good news is that there are many highly qualified professionals who can help you find your way through the labyrinth of Spanish bureaucracy and round the seemingly endless paperwork.

FINDING A JOB

The key to finding a good job in Spain is personal contact – this is a country where the right connections go a long way towards finding you employment. Casual jobs and jobs at the bottom of the employment ladder are relatively easy to find, particularly in areas where unemployment is low, e.g. Madrid and northern Spain, but if you aspire to more, you need to know people.

Many expatriates find it difficult and frustrating to break into the job market because a large proportion of vacancies are filled through personal recommendation or internally within a company.

Although it obviously helps more if your father is best mates with the director, personal contact works at all levels, however low, and networking is very important. Make sure your name, face and aspirations are well known: visit companies in person to hand in your CV; phone a few days later to follow up your application; be prepared to attend an interview at any time; and make sure all your friends and acquaintances know what sort of job you're looking for and what your qualifications are.

Speaking Spanish

Unless you plan to work solely within the expat community, where your job and career possibilities are severely limited, you need to speak reasonable Spanish. Outside popular expat destinations, there are virtually no job opportunities for non-Spanish speakers other than manual labour such as fruit picking. The better your Spanish is, the better your employment prospects.

Qualifications

In theory, any EU qualification is recognised in Spain; in practice the 'validation' process (*convalidación*)

Writing a CV

Any CV submitted in Spain should be in Spanish as well as in English (which is considered an asset for most jobs) – have yours professionally translated even if you think your Spanish is 'perfect'. Put your contact details at the top and tailor the contents to the job application, listing experience, skills and qualifications relevant to the job only. Include your date of birth and nationality, and limit the CV to two sides of A4.

> If you apply by letter or email, it's always wise to follow up with a telephone call. The Spanish are notoriously bad at committing anything to paper, but this is for the simple reason that they would much rather talk to you, on the telephone or, preferably, face to face.

is tangled in red tape and typically takes several months (at least). If your job hunting success depends on your qualifications being recognised, apply for validation well in advance of your arrival in Spain – Spanish consulates provide information on the process. It may be some consolation to know that it isn't just foreigners who have to go through this – newspapers frequently include letters from Spaniards who have achieved high qualifications abroad but have been unable to obtain recognition of these in their own country.

Employment Agencies

Government

It may come as a surprise to discover that the official employment agencies (run by regional governments under the umbrella of the Instituto Nacional de Empleo/ INEM) do relatively little to help you find a job. Offices post job vacancies – you're expected to browse through these – and if you're registered as unemployed you may receive the occasional phone call from the agency with details of a job offer, but don't expect to. Some agencies are better than others

and in the recent decentralisation process, regional governments have implemented measures to try to make the agencies more 'unemployed-friendly', but you cannot rely on an agency to find a job for you: the onus is on you to do your own job hunting.

Private

Head-hunting and recruitment agencies exist in Spain, although to a lesser extent than in the UK and US, but their activities are mainly confined to Barcelona and Madrid. Other agencies tend to deal only in temporary employment (*empresas de trabajo temporal*) and most large towns and cities have several, including the multi-nationals Adecco and Manpower. Several expat employment agencies are now active in Spain and specialise in finding employment (mainly on the Costa del Sol and in Gibraltar) for foreigners fluent in at least English and Spanish.

Selection Process

The job selection process in Spain usually involves several tests and interviews, particularly if you're applying for employment in a

large company. The tests (*tests psicológicos*) are used to ascertain your intelligence, aptitude (for a particular job) and personality: some companies expect candidates to sit several tests, which range from multiple-choice to essay format.

Some employers set tests before interviewing candidates – large companies tend to rule out 80 per cent of job applicants based on their CVs and test results – but others test after the interview stage.

The number of interviews you have depends on the company (and your success at interview), but expect at least two and possibly as many as seven. A surprising number of employers don't ask for references from your previous employers, but most want to see copies of your qualifications (these should be translated into Spanish).

Salary

Unless you're lucky enough to secure an executive post, where salaries are on a par with those in northern Europe, the chances are that your wages in Spain will be lower than in your home country. The legal minimum wage is around €570 per month (one of the lowest in the EU) and many salaries aren't a lot higher – a surprisingly large number of jobs (even skilled) offer a maximum gross salary of €1,000 per month and in some areas of Spain, such as the Costa del Sol, it's difficult to earn more. Spain's workforce consists of millions of employees known as *mileuristas* (€1,000-earners). On the plus side, employees receive 14 salary payments a year – two extra 'months' (*paga extraordinaria*) are paid: one at Christmas and one before the August summer holiday.

Salary Payments

Salaries are generally paid directly into your bank account at the beginning of every month (manual workers receive weekly payments). You sign and keep a copy of your salary slip (*nómina*), a complex document detailing your gross payment, tax deductions and social security payments. Any extra payments such as overtime, long service (*antigüedad*) and three-year bonus (*trienios*) are also listed.

When you receive your first salary slip, ask an expert to talk you through it and check that you're receiving the right amount.

> When buying a lease, negotiate the longest possible term – normally between 5 and 20 years. During the term of a lease your landlord can raise the rent only in line with inflation, but when a lease is renewed he's free to increase it by any amount.

Discrimination

Under Spanish law, racial and sexual discrimination is prohibited, meaning that theoretically anyone who meets the employment criteria has an equal chance of getting a job. In practice, this isn't always the case: Spain is 'a man's world' and a country where employers are still sometimes reluctant to take on young married women (for fear they'll fall pregnant and go on maternity leave), coloured people (racial prejudice runs deep in some company veins) and gypsies (many Spaniards are prejudiced against gypsies). White European men generally encounter no discrimination.

If you think a job wasn't awarded to you owing to discrimination, you have the right to appeal, but your case may be extremely difficult to prove.

CONTRACTS

Spanish labour law strongly favours the employee, and once a worker has signed an indefinite contract (*contrato fijo*) it's difficult and costly for an employer to fire him.

Not surprisingly, this means that employers tend to favour temporary or short-term contracts (*contrato indefinido* or *contrato temporal*) – with over a third of the workforce on short-term contracts Spain has the highest incidence of temporary employment in the EU.

Employment contracts are highly specific: they usually include a precise job description and detailed employment conditions (e.g. hours, pay and holiday entitlement)

and state the date from which they take effect. Contracts are binding on both parties and are important documents (keep a copy in a safe place in case of any dispute).

Collective Agreements

Employment conditions are wholly or partly determined by collective agreements (*convenios*), approved annually between management and unions. Collective agreements, which cover working conditions and salary scales, exist for almost every type of job in Spain.

STARTING OR BUYING A BUSINESS

The secret to setting up a business in Spain is research and more research together with a generous dose of patience as you plough through the inevitable red tape. Don't be tempted to by-pass the bureaucracy and start trading without registering and obtaining the necessary permissions. This is illegal and you'll probably be found out – there's a good chance that a competitor will report you; why should you get away with it when they did things properly? The authorities impose large fines on illegal traders and you'll find it difficult or impossible to set up a business afterwards.

Most foreign entrepreneurs find that financing a business in Spain is the most difficult part of setting up, more so than the paperwork. Even an extensive business plan for a potentially highly profitable business won't necessarily tempt financial institutions into lending you money to get it going.

Loans

Spanish banks are among the world's most cautious and aren't keen to lend to businesses. Foreigners are even less likely than Spaniards to receive approval for a business loan – even those who are resident and have some collateral (e.g. a property in Spain). Business plans need to be detailed and cover every conceivable aspect of a proposed business; some banks want to see 'evidence' that it's viable – a tall order if you're at the setting-up stage. Most banks require a guarantor, but sometimes even a multi-millionaire behind you isn't enough. This is one area in business where personal contacts aren't effective, as branch managers don't

Dali's calculator?

have the authority to approve loans – this is done at regional level.

If you do manage to squeeze a loan out of a bank, the repayment period will be relatively short (between five and seven years) and interest rates are likely to be high.

Grants

In theory, grants are available at many levels including EU, national, regional, provincial and local. In practice, tracking these down and actually receiving the money in your bank account is another matter altogether. The application process typically takes months, if not years, and there are numerous incidences of grants arriving several years after a business was set up. It's worth requesting as many grants as you're eligible for, but don't factor the grant money into your financing.

Premises

Most business premises (*locales*) are leased or rented – buying a commercial property is uncommon,

> Spain's black economy has embraced €500 notes with open arms and over a quarter of those in the euro zone 'circulate' in Spain (compared to 17 per cent in Italy and 39 per cent in Germany, both countries with much larger populations) – mostly under the table; the vast majority of Spaniards have never seen one.

not least because they're usually prohibitively expensive.

Leasing

Buying a lease (*cesión*, until recently known as a *traspaso*) is the most common way of acquiring premises and similar to renting (see below) except that a leaseholder has the right to sell his lease. When you buy a lease, you make a one-off payment, which includes fixtures and fittings, and then pay the property owner a monthly rental. When you sell the lease, you must give the landlord first refusal (*derecho de tanteo y retracto*) and he will normally take between 10 and 20 per cent commission from the sale – the amount should be stated in your contract.

Renting

The initial outlay when renting is cheaper than leasing and tenants with watertight contracts enjoy considerable rights, and it's difficult for a landlord to evict them. On the other hand, rental contracts are usually for one year at a time and at the end of the rental period you have no asset to sell on.

Working from Home

Under Spanish law you cannot set up just any business in your home: there are extensive regulations (and paperwork) concerning what you're permitted to do. Broadly speaking, many are designed with neighbours in mind and activities that interfere with 'normal' life are prohibited or restricted. This being Spain, however, rules and regulations vary from one municipality to another – some councils allow some businesses in some areas while others don't allow any. If you're considering working from home, visit your local council planning department (*departamento de urbanismo*) and find out the local regulations.

Self-employment

As in many countries, being self-employed in Spain is financially wearing, particularly at the beginning when you're setting up a business. Social security payments must be made monthly irrespective of your earnings and benefits are few (basic retirement pension, free public healthcare, and maternity leave) and low – most are based on a percentage of the minimum salary and not on your earnings, as is the case for employees. Income tax (20 per cent on all earnings after deduction of allowed expenses) must be declared and paid every quarter.

Although many self-employed people, especially those who are

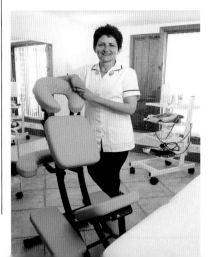

starting out, are entitled to high tax refunds when they make their annual declaration, this means that they've been deprived of the money for a year.

Marketing

In Spain a good reputation is a far more productive marketing tool than any number of adverts or expensive publicity campaigns and when most Spaniards need something they ask around for a recommendation.

Business contacts are therefore the key to professional success. Most professionals and businesses spend time networking and nurturing their contacts – good ones are taken out for coffee and lunch and phoned regularly. Have plenty of business cards and hand these out at every opportunity.

BLACK ECONOMY

After Italy, Spain is estimated to have the largest 'black' economy in the developed world. This isn't surprising given that the Spanish generally view the state as a rule

maker whose objective is to make life as difficult as possible for them (in the face of Spanish bureaucracy it's hard to disagree) and therefore believe it their 'duty' to commit tax fraud.

> 'The number of women in the professions has steadily increased over the years in line with the increase in the number of women graduates (who now outnumber male graduates), but only 4 per cent of senior management positions are held by women.'

The black economy operates at all levels, among both employers and workers – paying in cash, declaring a percentage of your income rather than all of it, invoicing for half a job but charging for all of it, employing unregistered workers, etc. It's difficult to live and work in Spain and not come across an aspect of the black economy, and many expats inevitably join in.

You may even find yourself part of the black economy unwittingly. If possible, however, you should avoid it – the authorities are clamping down on illegal activity, particularly in employment and tax declaration.

Note also that if you accept illegal employment you have no rights and are entitled to no benefits.

WORKING WOMEN

The number of working women has increased considerably over the last 20 years and nearly 50 per cent of Spanish women now work full- or part-time (almost 80 per cent of part-time workers are women). On the other hand, women account for two-thirds of Spain's unemployed and, owing to the fact that fewer women than men are in the employment market, female unemployment is twice as high as that of men.

Sexual discrimination is prohibited and a woman doing the same or broadly similar work to a man and employed by the same employer is legally entitled to the same salary and other terms of employment. However, it's estimated that women earn up to a third less than men in similar posts.

New legislation was introduced in 2006 with measures designed to improve sexual equality in the workplace, and the government is working hard to change attitudes.

> 'Spain is a people place; you've got to have a personal relationship with someone before anything happens.'
>
> Adela Gooch (Spanish correspondent)

However, Spain's 'macho' culture means that many men resent having a female boss, particularly a foreign one, and women generally have to go the extra mile to prove themselves in the workplace. If you're a woman employed in a management position, try to establish your credentials and abilities as soon as possible – once you've earned your colleagues' respect, their attitudes and cooperation will improve dramatically. Dress modestly and avoid anything that may be interpreted as flirting or showing interest in a male colleague.

BUSINESS ETIQUETTE

In the workplace, as in any other environment, there are unwritten rules that must be observed if you're to avoid upsetting others – particularly Spaniards – and be accepted by your colleagues and clients.

Appointments

Don't expect to see anyone in Spain without an appointment – even those with empty diaries will have a full agenda of invented activities when you turn up unexpectedly to see them. Make an appointment at least a week in advance, preferably by telephone or fax, and, if you cannot make it or are going to be late, let the person know.

Business Cards

Business cards are essential and an integral part of Spain's networking culture. Choose the best you can afford – the Spanish like to see an elegant, well designed card – and make sure it's in Spanish (though you may have English on the other side). Cards may be exchanged at the beginning or end of a meetingand everyone present expects to receive one. You should also leave one with the receptionist when you arrive for a meeting.

> If a meeting is in English, speak slowly and clearly until you gauge the other person's level of English. Even if it's high, avoid using idioms such as 'a New York minute' or 'the ball's in your court' – few foreigners will understand these – and beware of using 'sloppy' English, e.g. 'wanna' and 'gonna', which also makes it difficult for non-native speakers to understand.

Business Gifts

Gifts are usually offered only when there has been some business success, e.g. signing a contract or agreement. If you decide it's appropriate to offer a gift and there's no risk of it being interpreted as a bribe, choose a high-quality item (but not too ostentatious) and make sure it's attractively wrapped.

Typical items from your home country, e.g. a bottle of Scotch whisky or a craft product, are safe bets, as are a good bottle of (Spanish) wine or an elegant pen or desk set.

When you're on the receiving end, it's polite to open a present as soon as you receive it.

Business Hours

The working day in Spain is long and in general you'll find that meals and other activities take place later than you're used to. Most employees start at 8 or 9am and work until 2 or 3pm, when there's a lunch break of two or three hours after which work resumes until 7 or 8pm, by which time you might expect to be fed and watered and watching the telly. Summer (usually 15th June to 15th September) working hours are condensed and tend to be 8am to 3pm. However, businesses are increasingly adapting to more 'European' working hours and many companies work all day (9am to 6pm) all year round.

Business Lunches

Lunches in Spain are long affairs and business lunches are no exception. However, business may not be discussed at all during the meal, which is usually seen as an opportunity to get to know a client or supplier. Don't start a business discussion with a Spaniard, but wait for him to do so. Expect the meal to last around two hours, typically from 2 to 4pm and for alcohol to be served and consumed. Cigars may be offered with coffee.

Dress

The Spanish dress formally and smartly for work and pay particular attention to accessories (i.e. shoes, ties and bags), which tend to be matching. It's best to dress conservatively – dark suits are the norm. Men wear ties and jackets, except in July and August in some companies. Women should dress smartly and avoid short skirts and low-cut tops – in Spain's prevailing macho society, this type of clothing may give the wrong signals to male colleagues or clients.

Meetings

Meetings in Spain are generally seen as an opportunity to exchange ideas and receive information. Few decisions are reached at a meeting as time is needed to mull over the ideas expressed before a decision can be made.

Agenda

Most meetings have an official agenda and you may receive a written copy of this. However, the agenda isn't cast in stone and may be followed roughly, in part, or not at all, depending on the course the meeting takes. Bringing the agenda to people's attention is considered rude.

> Like time, deadlines are flexible: they're usually met, but not always. However, the fact that something arrives a few days late isn't a cause for concern but is accepted as part of normal business life. In recent years, however, Spanish businesses (in their bid for improved competitiveness) have become much better at keeping to schedule.

First Meetings

Spaniards like to do business with people they know and trust, and they consider that the key to successful business dealings is a solid personal relationship. Few Spaniards do business with someone they've met briefly or know little about. First meetings are therefore used mainly for getting to know each other and often taken up entirely with building the foundations of a relationship, rather than actual business. Don't be surprised, therefore, if most of an initial meeting is taken up with 'small talk' and don't try to force a business agenda at the first encounter. Take the initiative from your host and follow his pace.

Language

English is widely spoken in some

parts of Spain and the ability to speak English is high on most Spaniards' wish list. However, you should never assume that a Spaniard can speak and/or understand English. Expect the meeting to take place in Spanish – take an interpreter with you if your Spanish isn't good enough. If you wish the meeting to be conducted in English, start by greeting the person in Spanish and politely ask if he speaks English – never start in English, as he may feel ridiculed if his English is poor.

> Since the advent of democracy, four general strikes have been called: the last, in 2002, was against government unemployment policy, which was changed after the strike brought most of the country to a standstill.

Negotiating

When negotiating a business deal with a Spaniard, bear in mind the following:

- The Spanish like to voice their opinions and often do so loudly and passionately (don't misinterpret passion for anger). They offer others the opportunity to express their opinions but may interrupt them in full flow.
- The Spanish have great respect for modesty and little for arrogance – be self-effacing in your descriptions of your company's achievements and products. An astute counterpart will pick up on this and hold you in higher esteem.
- Talking about money-making and how much profit you expect to gain is considered bad taste.
- Never criticise anyone at a meeting – Spaniards abhor public humiliation. Keep your negative opinions to yourself.
- Don't expect a decision to be reached at a meeting: management usually takes a decision afterwards and in private.
- All business dealings are based on mutual trust, therefore a Spanish client might prefer to make a small initial order to see whether you fulfil expectations, before taking things further.
- Be patient at all stages of negotiation: Spaniards hate rushing (except when they're behind a steering wheel) and dislike others hurrying them. Accept that each stage takes time.
- Once an agreement is reached, Spaniards expect both sides to adhere to it. Oral agreements (sealed with a handshake) are still considered by some to be just as valid as written contracts.

Regional Differences

The huge cultural differences

between the regions of Spain are also present in business, and your experience with a Catalan company may be a world away from the way you're dealt with by a business in Seville. In general the north of Spain – particularly the Basque Country and Catalonia, Spain's industrial and commercial powerhouses – has a more northern European work ethic and the south of Spain, a more Latin, Mediterranean style, but don't take this for granted.

You also need to be prepared for huge contrasts in business styles and operations between different companies: Spain is home to dynamic, modern businesses based on US models using the latest technology and management policies, but also to small, traditional companies, often family-run, where little has changed in decades.

These contrasts mean that foreigners intending to do business in Spain need to be adaptable and flexible – if in doubt about how to proceed, wait for the key figures on the Spanish side to take the initiative.

Timekeeping

Timekeeping and punctuality are relative concepts in Spain, where few events (other than the most important things in life, such as bullfights and football matches) start at their advertised time. However, if you're trying to sell a product or service, you should arrive on time – or even five or ten minutes early. This shows that you're serious (*serio*) and wish to be taken seriously. If you're going to be late,

Agbar Tower, Barcelona

you should phone and say so. Don't expect your counterpart to be on time, however – 15 to 30 minutes late is considered acceptable – and, unless he's extremely late, don't expect an apology or explanation

EMPLOYING PEOPLE

Think long and hard before you employ staff in Spain – it's no exaggeration to say that you'll be stepping into the proverbial minefield. Spanish labour law is one of the most rigid in the Western world and employees with indefinite contracts are among the best protected. Labour legislation is designed to protect employees from

> Oral agreements are valid under Spanish law, and if you pay someone for work you're deemed to have entered into a contractual relationship even if there's no written contract.

exploitation and they therefore enjoy extensive rights – to the extent that many employers complain **they** are the exploited ones and have fewer rights than their employees. Workers are entitled to a minimum wage, 14 'monthly' payments, one month's paid holiday and 14 paid public holidays.

> Spain uses the metric system for everything (except TV screen-sizes, which are stated in inches) so you should quote in kilos/metres/litres/centigrade/etc.

Contracts

Be wary of entering into a permanent contract (*contrato fijo* or *indefinido*) with an employee unless you're sure he's the right person for the job and has proved his worth in your business. Employees on permanent contracts are extremely difficult to fire (unless they commit a heinous crime) and if a court rules that the dismissal is unfair – which they usually do – employers must pay huge compensation, e.g. 45 days' salary for each year of service.

Domestic Help

As in many countries, the vast majority of workers employed in homes, e.g. gardeners and cleaners, work illegally, as few 'employers' offer them contracts and pay their social security contributions as they should. You should be wary of doing this, however, as it isn't uncommon for a maid or gardener to report their employer for not making social security contributions.

If you employ someone illegally in your home and he has an accident, you're considered responsible and liable for damages – which can be astronomical.

Social Security

Social security contributions can be financially crippling for a new business – an employer must pay around 24 per cent of each employee's gross pay, the employee paying only around 4 per cent.

Tax

You're responsible for making monthly deductions for income tax (withholding tax) from an employee's salary and for providing a monthly payslip (*nómina*) and annual 'certificate of deducted tax' (*certificado de retenciones*).

TRADE UNIONS

Spain doesn't have a strong trade union (*sindicato*) movement and only some 13 per cent of the workforce belong to a union. Nevertheless, the two main union confederations, the socialist Unión General de Trabajadores (UGT) and the Communist Comisiones Obreras (CCOO), play a major role in industrial negotiations such as collective labour agreements (*convenios*) and are key players in national employment policy. Trade unions celebrate Labour Day (1st May) with demonstrations and parades in most cities and large towns throughout the country.

Industrial relations have improved hugely over the last few years – during the '80s Spain had one of the worst industrial records in Europe – and in 2005 there were 'only' around 680 strikes (down 23 per cent on 2004).

Joining a Union

Employees aren't obliged to join unions, but all businesses with 50 or more employees are required to have some sort of employee representation. The benefits of joining a union include free access to legal services, job training programmes and subsidised holidays and children's summer camps. Membership costs from €10 per month and is tax-deductible.

WORKING WEEK

The typical Spanish working week is 40 hours from Monday to Friday. In the past, Saturday was also part of the working week and it's still officially considered a working day (*día laborable*) and Sunday the only official day off in the week – Sundays and public holidays are shown in red on calendars.

Coffee Breaks

Few companies have scheduled coffee breaks, but most employees are entitled to 30 minutes off during the morning and during the afternoon for coffee. This explains why it's difficult to find a civil servant behind a desk between 10 and 11am.

HOLIDAYS

Employees are generally entitled to one month's holiday a year plus public holidays. The vast majority of workers take the whole of a month off, usually during July or August, and very few split their annual leave into shorter holidays. August is the most popular month for holidays and if you're a new arrival in a company you're unlikely to be able to take your holiday during this month unless the entire company or business closes (as is common in manufacturing and industry). Choice of when you take your holiday is decided by strict hierarchy, those at the top getting first pick.

The Spanish take their holidays

seriously and the vast majority of employees take all their annual leave – foregoing part of your holiday in order to work is virtually unheard of. There are certain times of the year in Spain when it's best to avoid doing business (see below); if you have to, expect things to take **even** longer than usual.

July & August

During the summer months many companies switch to a continuous working day (typically 8am to 3pm).

It's common for companies to close down in August, and those that stay open often operate on a skeleton staff as most employees are taking their annual holiday.

Christmas & Easter

The festive period, which in Spain lasts until 7th January, and Holy Week (the week including Good Friday, not the following week) are peak holiday periods and best avoided if you want to do any business.

Public Holidays

One of the best things about being an employee in Spain is the number of public holidays, which crop up regularly throughout the year to a total of 14, the highest in Europe. Only ten are celebrated nationally (see below), the remaining four being made up of Maundy Thursday or Easter Monday, one regional and two local holidays – with the result that there's a public holiday somewhere in Spain more or less every day of the year.

> A Eurostat survey in 2006 found that the average working week in Spain is 38.2 hours, compared with the EU average of 36.3 hours.

Date	Holiday
1st January	New Year's Day (*Día del Año Nuevo*)
6th January	Epiphany or Three Kings Day (*Día de los Reyes Magos*)
March/April	Good Friday (*Viernes Santo*)
1st May	Labour Day (*Día del Trabajador*)
15th August	Assumption of the Virgin (*Asunción*)
12th October	Virgin of Pilar/National Day (*Día de Virgen del Pilar*)
1st November	All Saints' Day (*Día de Todos los Santos*)
6th December	Constitution Day (*Día de la Constitución*)
8th December	Immaculate Conception (*Inmaculada Concepción*)
25th December	Christmas Day (*Día de Navidad*)

When a holiday falls on a Saturday, another day isn't granted as a holiday, but if it falls on a Sunday, the following Monday is a public holiday. When a public holiday falls on a Tuesday or Thursday, the Monday or Friday is usually declared a holiday as well, although this depends on the employer. This practice is called making a bridge (*hacer un puente*). If a holiday falls on a Wednesday, employees may take the two preceding or succeeding days off, a practice known as making a viaduct (*viaducto*). When two public holidays fall midweek (e.g. 6th and 8th December), many people take the whole week off (known as a *superpuente*).

All public offices, banks and post offices are closed on public holidays and only essential work is performed. Foreign embassies and consulates in Spain usually observe all Spanish public holidays, **as well as** their own country's national holidays.

Local Holidays

Many localities have week-long celebrations and one of the days is a public holiday. During the rest of the week local businesses including banks and public offices open for shorter hours (e.g. 9am to midday), known as *horario de feria*. Trying to do business during *feria* week is usually a waste of time as few people are in the mood for work.

Special Leave

All employees are entitled to additional days off for certain occasions, e.g. moving house (one day), marriage (one day), and the death of a family member (two days). Maternity and paternity leave are also granted. Employees aren't allocated a number of days a year for sick leave as is common in some countries. If you're sick, the correct procedure is to contact your workplace first thing in the morning of the first day you're unable to go to work. If you're ill for more than two days, you need a medical certificate (*certificado médico*) from your doctor.

Consuegra, Toledo

7.

ON THE MOVE

Spanish cities and large towns usually have good and cheap public transport networks and there are excellent nationwide bus, plane and train services. But to travel from A to B, Spaniards inevitably get their cars out and the chances are that you'll be joining them. To help reduce the surprise (and possibly shock) factor of driving in Spain, this chapter contains useful tips, including road rules, driving etiquette and where to park, as well as information on getting around on public transport.

> It's important to drive defensively in Spain and always expect the unexpected from Spanish drivers.

SAFETY

Spain is generally a safe country to travel in, but bear in mind the following:

- **Petty thieves** – These are rife on public transport in large cities, particularly Madrid and Barcelona, and crowded buses and trains are favourite targets. Hold your belongings in front of you – wear rucksacks on your chest – and if possible, keep your money, ID and house keys in an inside pocket or money belt.

- **Automatic doors on trains** – Alarms sound on train and metro doors when they're within a few seconds of closing. Don't attempt to board or leave when you hear this sound.

- **Late-night train travel** – If you travel on the train or metro late at night, board a carriage near the driver or with several other passengers in it.

- **Bus and train stations** – these are best avoided late at night because many become drug-pusher and drug-user territory. If you can't avoid them, stay near members of staff or manned ticket offices. If you're due to arrive late at night, ask someone to meet you.

- **Unlicensed taxis** – Beware of unlicensed taxis in main cities preying on foreign visitors – these are particularly common in Alicante and Barcelona. If you aren't sure, ask to see the licence number **before** you get in.

- **Single women** – you may feel safer sitting in the back of a taxi. On a train at night, travel in the carriage next to the guard's or driver's van.

- **Hitchhiking** – It's legal in Spain, although not as common as it was, and generally safe, although women should avoid it.

DRIVING

Driving on Spanish roads isn't for the faint-hearted and although Spanish drivers aren't the worst in Europe, they give the Italians and Portuguese a good run for their money and make French drivers seem like paragons of virtue. Spain has one of the worst accident records in the EU with 28 deaths per kilometre travelled by 10,000 cars (the EU average is 13) and in 2005 an average of 12 people were killed on the roads **every day**.

The death-wish unruliness that characterises Spaniards' driving seems to go against their relaxed *mañana* attitude but is part of the underlying culture of recklessness in Spain, where more than a third of drivers regularly don't wear a seatbelt – the irrepressible urge to run in front of a charging bull is also symptomatic of this attitude.

The traffic authorities frequently run high-impact advertising campaigns designed to reduce the accident rate. The adverts often include shocking images – one in 2006 showed an unseatbelted child hurtling through a windscreen. Recent slogans include '*Lo importante es volver*' ('The most

important thing is to get home'), shown on illuminated signs during holiday periods, and '*No podemos conducir por ti*' ('We cannot drive for you'), appealing to drivers to behave more responsibly on the roads. It isn't yet known whether these have had any effect.

Drivers

Like all Latins, Spaniards seem to change personality the moment they get behind the wheel of a car, when even normally tolerant and patient people turn into suicidal maniacs. Many Spaniards are frustrated racing drivers and they rush around at breakneck speed in their haste to reach their destination (or the next life). To many male Spaniards, driving is like a bullfight and an opportunity to demonstrate their *machismo* to their wives and girlfriends – or just about anyone.

Foreign-registered cars (observing speed limits) are like red rags to a bull to some Spaniards, who must overtake them immediately, irrespective of their speed, the speed limit, road markings, weather

> What's the definition of a nano-second in Spain? The time between a traffic light turning green and the driver behind hooting.

conditions or oncoming traffic. For many male drivers (in the first three months of the new points system, 87 per cent of offenders were male), the only thing that matters on the road is to get in front of the car immediately ahead of them.

Tailgating (i.e. driving too close for comfort to the car in front) is a favourite pastime among male drivers and many sit almost in your boot, trying to push you along irrespective of traffic density, road and weather conditions, or the speed limit. To intimidate you further, they put their indicators on, flash their lights and hoot. If you cannot (or refuse to) budge, they will invariably cut you up – on the outside or the inside or even the hard shoulder. If you're in front of a tailgater, leave a large gap between you and the vehicle in front – this gives you and the tailgater extra space for an emergency stop.

Among the many motoring 'idiosyncrasies' you'll encounter are a total lack of lane discipline (lane markings are treated as suggestions); overtaking with reckless abandon on blind bends; failure to use mirrors or indicators (especially when changing lanes); jumping red lights; and driving the wrong way up one-way streets.

Spanish Roads

Spanish roads have improved greatly over the last decade, but although

drivers have the opportunity to drive along some of the best motorways in Europe – quiet, wide and smooth – they also have to contend with some of the worst. In 2006 two independent reports found that around a third of Spain's roads were in poor condition and that 13km of every 100km of road are dangerous.

Rural roads are the worst offenders – pot holes, dips, tight corners and hairpin bends are commonplace – but poor surfaces and narrowing (or disappearing) lanes are found everywhere. Beware of mountain roads in Spain – there are many and most rise to dizzying heights. They are also narrow (often not wide enough for two vehicles to pass), winding and sheer drops on one side, which barriers do little to protect you from. Progress along these is slow and not for those who suffer from nerves or vertigo, although the spectacular views often compensate.

Spain has several toll roads (*autopista de peaje*), which provide a quick and relatively safe means of travelling long-distance, but they're expensive and junctions are

> Take extra care on mountain roads and be sure to keep well over to your own side of the road on blind corners.

few and far between. Toll roads are identified by the letters *AP* and the word '*peaje*' enclosed within a circle outlined in red. The signs are often small and many drivers are caught out and find themselves on a toll road by accident.

Road Rules

Study the Spanish highway code (*Código de Circulación* – available from newsagents and bookshops) before you take to the roads so

> Hazard warning lights are commonly used to warn vehicles behind of a hazard ahead, e.g. an accident or a slow-moving vehicle, and as a sign when you're illegally parked that you'll be back in a minute and a plea for the police to turn a blind eye (most do). Needless to say, only the former use is approved.

you know what all the signs mean. Among the most important points are:

● The Spanish drive on the right-hand side of the road, which means you go anti-clockwise round roundabouts.

● Speed limits are 120kph (75mph) on motorways (*autopistas*); 100kph (62mph) on dual-carriageways (*autovías*) and other main roads (*carreteras*); 50kph (31mph) in built-up areas (*vías urbanas*) or as signposted.

● All occupants must wear a seatbelt and children under 12 aren't allowed in the front seat.

● The use of a mobile (unless it's a

hands-free set without earphones) is prohibited.

● White lines are used for traffic lanes. A solid single line means no overtaking – you can overtake only when there's a single broken line or double lines with a broken line on your side of the road.

● To turn left, you must usually use a central filter lane or turn right into a filter lane and stop and wait for both lanes to clear of traffic before you cross. Only on minor roads are you allowed to stop in your lane and wait to turn left.

● According to the highway code, the horn is for emergency use only, but Spanish drivers make optimum use of it, especially when they're in a traffic jam or desperate to overtake the vehicle in front.

● Under Spanish law, you must carry the following in your vehicle: two hazard warning triangles; a reflective waistcoat; a full set of spare bulbs and fuses; all car documentation including proof of insurance cover; your driving licence; a spare wheel and tools for changing a wheel. It's also recommended that you carry a first aid kit, fire extinguisher and set of snow chains (except in August in Marbella).

Points System

Spain introduced a points system in July 2006: drivers are awarded an initial 'score' of 12 points (new drivers only eight) and when an offence is committed points are deducted (fines are also payable, ranging from €90 to €1,500) as follows:

- **Six points** – drunk driving (over 50mg per 100ml); refusing to take a breath test; speeding at 50 per cent over the limit; dangerous driving.

- **Four points** – speeding at more than 40kph over the limit; drunk driving (over 25mg per 100ml); jumping a 'give way', 'stop' sign or a red light; throwing rubbish out of the car; dangerous overtaking; putting a cyclist in danger when overtaking him.

- **Three points** – failure to maintain a safe distance between the vehicle in front; driving between 30 to 40kph over the limit; driving without lights in poor visibility conditions; using a mobile phone or headphones while driving; not wearing a seatbelt or helmet.

- **Two points** – stopping on bends or tunnels; driving between 20 to 30kph over the speed limit.

In the first three months after the system was introduced, drivers in Spain lost nearly 215,000 points between them, driving standards improved noticeably and the death rate fell by 30 per cent.

Finding Your Way

Spanish drivers are among the world's most unforgiving if you're lost in a city. Trying to change lane or read the name of a street before deciding whether to turn off prompts a tirade of horn sounding, shouting and rude gestures from drivers behind you. Study a map thoroughly before you venture out, invest in a GPS unit or take a taxi.

> The long break for lunch means Spain is unique in having four rush hours (horas puntas): 8 to 9.30am, 12.30 to 2.30pm, 4 to 5pm and 6.30 to 8.30pm; the quietest periods are usually between 3 and 4pm and late at night. Traffic jams are particularly bad in cities such as Madrid and Barcelona, where the rush 'hour' lasts all day.

Motorcyclists & Pedestrians

Keep a sharp eye out for motorcyclists, who often overtake on the inside, particularly in towns, and between cars in the outside lane and the crash barrier on motorways.

Watch out too for pedestrians – many have kamikaze tendencies and start crossing the road without looking or step off the pavement in front of you. Pedestrian crossings (*pasos de peatones*) consist of black

and white or red and white stripes on the road, sometimes with a traffic light. You aren't obliged to stop at a crossing unless the light is red or there's a pedestrian already on it; if you decide to do so, make sure you look in your mirror first, as the driver behind won't be expecting it and could plough into your boot.

Roundabouts

Many Spanish drivers haven't got to grips with roundabouts – they're a relatively new arrival on the scene – and most don't indicate, some don't give way before entering a roundabout, some give way to traffic coming onto it and some treat roundabouts as if they weren't a junction at all and drive straight across them. Take extra care on roundabouts and be prepared for anything to happen.

Traffic Jams

Finding yourself stuck in a long queue of traffic is inevitable if you drive anywhere near a built-up area in Spain. Traffic jams (*atascos*) are caused by accidents, 'rubber-neckers' slowing down to gawp at an accident, too many cars on the road (particularly in rush hours), double-parked vehicles, buses collecting passengers (and forced to stop on the road because the bus stop is full of parked cars), friends passing the time of day… but patience isn't a Spanish driving virtue and jams in towns and cities are noisy affairs as most drivers sit on their horns in protest. No one will mind if you join them, but the cacophony rarely makes the traffic move any faster.

Better to avoid rush hours (easier said than done – see below) or find an alternative route.

Parking

Given the large number of cars and small number of streets in most Spanish towns and cities, it isn't surprising to discover that finding a parking space is both challenging and time-consuming. Some Spaniards solve the problem creatively (and quickly) by parking anywhere – any space large enough for a car is deemed a parking spot – and pavements, bus stops and driveways are often crowded with parked cars.

> In many self-service petrol stations and all stations open after 11pm, you must pay before you fill up. When filling up with petrol, you must turn off the engine, all lights, electrical equipment (including the radio) and your mobile phone.

Official parking spaces include underground car parks – your best bet as they're easy to find and secure, but parking is expensive; 'blue zones' (*zonas azules*), where you take a ticket from a machine and maximum parking time is

between 90 and 120 minutes; streets without no-parking signs (e.g. yellow or red lines on kerb, or a blue sign with a red line through it). A practical alternative is to park in the outskirts and walk or bus into the centre. Spain has no 'park and ride' facilities as are common in the UK.

> Avoid driving into the centre of small towns and villages – you may find yourself in a labyrinth of narrow one-way streets, the only exit being down a flight of steps...

Double Parking

Returning to your car and finding that someone has parked beside it, preventing you from going anywhere, is common. If it happens to you, the conventional procedure is to sound your horn continuously until the owner of the other car appears. This could be a while as he may be in a bank or shopping, but if you've sounded your horn for more than 15 minutes to no avail, call the local police and ask for the offending vehicle to be towed away.

Parking Illegally

If you return to your parking space and your car isn't there, the chances are it has been towed away (or stolen). In some cities, tow truck drivers leave a sticker (indicating your number plate) next to where you were parked, but usually you have to phone the local police and ask. The car pound is usually a taxi ride away and getting your car back will cost between €50 and €120 plus the parking fine (and the taxi).

Petrol Stations

Petrol stations (*gasolineras*) are plentiful throughout most of Spain but few and far between in some rural areas. Some are self-service (*autoservicio*) but many are manned (*servicio atendido*) – this is written on the side of the petrol pumps.

Check first because attendants get worked up if you operate a pump yourself. You don't need to tip an attendant unless he washes your windscreen or checks your tyre pressure, when you should leave €1 or €2. Petrol stations have tyre pressure pumps and water supplies, and some have vacuum cleaners and car washes. Many stations sell snacks, drinks, newspapers, confectionary, cigarettes, local produce such as cheeses and sacks of oranges, and car accessories including oil. Toilets are available, but standards of cleanliness vary from acceptable to better-hang-on-until-you-get-home. Toilet paper and soap are rare commodities.

PUBLIC TRANSPORT

A few general points apply to most types of public transport:

● Online and telephone bookings

can be made with most large transport companies, but not all.

- Travel by long-distance train, by ferry and on domestic flights is cheaper between midday Monday and Thursday evening.

- In July and August and at other peak holiday times – Christmas, Easter and national holidays – book a seat well in advance.

- Food and drink on trains and planes is expensive and mediocre.

- Smoking is prohibited at airports, at bus and train stations, on public transport and on domestic flights.

Taxis

Taxis are common in large towns and cities, and are usually white with a coloured stripe and local emblem (e.g. coat of arms) on the sides. A notable exception is Barcelona taxis – black with a yellow stripe. You can order a taxi by phone (*radio taxi*), go to a taxi rank (*parada de taxi*) - where you should ask which taxi is first in the queue to take passengers – or hail one in the street by signalling with an outstretched arm (a '*libre*' sign in the windscreen or a green light on the roof indicates that a taxi is free). Taxis are cheap in Spain – a recent survey found they're among the cheapest in Europe. Tariffs within urban areas

are calculated by a meter, but journeys outside urban areas usually have fixed prices and it's best to agree one with the driver before you start a journey. It isn't usual to tip a taxi driver, but many passengers round the fare up to the nearest euro or banknote.

> 'There's nothing like an airport for bringing you down to earth.'
>
> Richard Gordon (Scottish TV presenter)

Planes

- Many Spanish airports are currently undergoing expansion – Alicante and Malaga are two examples – so allow extra time for check-in.

- Terminal 4 (T4) at Madrid's Barajas airport is some distance from the other terminals and cannot be reached by public transport so if you have a flight or connecting flight in T4 allow extra time for your journey.

- Residents of the Balearics and Canaries are entitled to between 33 and 38 per cent discount on flights between the islands and the mainland, and on inter-island flights.

- Flight and general information at large airports is usually given

in Spanish and English (and sometimes German). At smaller airports, information is in Spanish only.

- Spanish internet travel portals don't always sell tickets on low-cost airlines, making it difficult to compare flight prices unless you visit low-cost airlines' websites individually.

Buses & Trains

- Spain doesn't have an extensive rail network and going by train isn't necessarily quicker than taking a bus or coach.

- Waiting rooms and toilet facilities at train and bus stations are often grim – use a local café or bar if you arrive early.

- On most trains you have to push a button to open the door. On metros, doors open and close automatically at stations.

- On long-distance trains, you're allocated a seat when you buy your ticket. On other trains, it's first-come, first-gets-a-seat.

- A return train ticket is between 20 and 40 per cent cheaper than a single.

- Spanish trains, particularly local services (*cercanías*), are generally

punctual. If you travel by *AVE* (high speed train) and arrive between 21 and 40 minutes late, you're entitled to a 25 per cent refund. If it's more than an hour late, you get your money back.

- Cancellations and date changes on bookings are possible, but you must pay between 10 and 15 per cent of the ticket price.

ON FOOT

Finally, a couple of notes about being a pedestrian in Spain:

- **Pedestrian crossings** – As motorists aren't obliged to stop at a pedestrian crossing unless the light is red or there's a pedestrian already on it, don't start crossing unless there's no traffic or oncoming cars have plenty of time to stop. Even if the light for cars is red and the green man is showing, check that traffic has stopped before you step out as drivers routinely jump red lights. If the traffic light is flashing amber, take extra care as drivers don't have to stop and many will drive around you as you cross.

- **Pavements** – Many footpaths or pavements (*aceras*) are obstacle courses, strewn with mopeds, bins, rubbish and, of course, parked cars. Street lights and signs are often placed 'conveniently' in the middle of pavements and you also need to keep an eye out for broken paving stones (loose, and full of dirty water, ready to soak your shoes and legs), open manholes and dog muck. If you have a pushchair or wheelchair, walking in the road is often an easier, if more dangerous, option.

8.
THE SPANISH AT PLAY

Becoming socially adept in a different culture is perhaps the greatest challenge in your bid to 'fit in' abroad, as you're most likely to do the wrong thing when socialising. To help you avoid social gaffes, this chapter contains information on dress code, dining out (and in), and sporting and leisure activities – as well as what to expect of Spanish toilets.

> Not for nothing is 'a vivir que son dos días' ('live it up because you've only got two days left') a regularly cited Spanish proverb.'

DRESS CODE

Your appearance is of the utmost importance in Spain, where making a good impression is among many Spaniards' priorities. Historically, in times of poverty many Spaniards preferred to go hungry rather than dress in rags and even today many people of modest means will spend a small fortune on an outfit for an important occasion such as a wedding or on a large car (usually bought on hire purchase), mainly for the sake of appearances.

Spanish men and women are almost invariably well groomed and in fashion, particularly in Madrid, which rivals Paris and Milan in 'street style'. In provincial capitals, where society tends to be close knit, few people go out without first making a big effort to look smart. In resort areas and more cosmopolitan cities (mainly those where the influence of tourists is greater, e.g. Malaga and Barcelona), appearance isn't so important and people tend to dress more casually. However, most Spaniards consider swimwear, skimpy tops and flip-flops strictly for the beach or pool and despair over the sloppy dress favoured by tourists, especially the British.

Home

Behind the closed front door of their home, many Spaniards dress in tracksuits or housecoats and slippers – outfits they wouldn't be seen dead in outside. This is another reason it isn't a good idea to turn up unannounced at a Spaniard's home.

Places of Worship

If you're wearing shorts and/or a skimpy top, you'll probably be refused entry into a place of worship. In some, such as major cathedrals, women are asked to cover the tops of their arms. In any case, it's a sign

of respect to dress modestly when entering a place of worship in Spain and you should do so irrespective of regulations.

Social Occasions

A social event provides a Spaniard with the perfect excuse to dress up to the nines and you may be surprised at the lengths the Spanish go to in preparation for a wedding or party.

Women think nothing of spending several hundred euros on an outfit with matching shoes and bag, and almost always go to the hairdressers' before an event. Men usually wear their best suit and tie. If you're invited to a social event and don't want to feel like an outcast, you should dress up.

Work

Most Spaniards dress smartly for work – a suit and tie command respect in many people – and a large number of professions have 'uniforms'. Office workers and bankers must usually wear a suit (and tie for men) and many companies forbid casual wear. Few workplaces prohibit trousers for women, but most businesses expect women to dress conservatively.

EATING

Like most Latins, Spaniards live to eat and one of the great pleasures of living in Spain is its abundance of inexpensive eating places serving excellent food. Eating out is a popular social activity and a source of great enjoyment – many Spaniards eat out on Sundays and public holidays, when restaurants are full to bursting – and you'll often see whole families, including three or four generations and children of all ages, dining together. Meals are long – lasting at least an hour and usually far more – and as much a social occasion as a means of filling your stomach. Portions are invariably large and meals normally include two main courses and dessert and coffee. Meals tend to be lighter in the south and heavier in the north, particularly in Asturias, the Basque Country and the north of Castilla y León, where huge plates of stew followed by enormous steaks or half a chicken are dished up as an everyday lunch.

> La Caixa's 2006 economic survey of Spain identified 328,202 bars and restaurants in Spain, Andalusia and Catalonia leading the way and each accounting for 16 per cent of the total.

During your stay in Spain you'll probably receive invitations to many meals in both informal and formal settings. Knowing which cutlery to use, what (not) to talk about and how to behave at table not only makes you feel more comfortable; it might make the difference between being invited again or not.

Meals

Breakfast

Spanish breakfast is usually of the continental type – coffee and toasted rolls served with olive oil or jam. Baguette sandwiches (*bocadillos*) with ham and cheese, *chorizo* or pâté are also popular, as are croissants.

Many Spaniards have breakfast in a bar or café at around 10am (breakfast at home is often little more than a rushed cup of coffee) and children take a sandwich to school for their mid-morning break.

Lunch

This is the main meal of the day and is eaten from 2pm onwards. Lunch traditionally consists of two main courses (the first course is usually more substantial than a starter) and dessert (usually fruit). A glass of wine or beer is often served. Many Spaniards eat lunch at home and return to work at 4 or 5pm. Those who don't lunch at home tend to go to restaurants or bars serving a *menú del día*. Most Spaniards consider it sacrilege to have anything other than a proper meal at lunchtime and few people eat sandwiches.

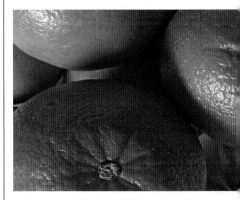

Merienda

The afternoon snack, known as a *merienda*, is an institution in Spanish children's lives and the ritual takes place every day at around 6pm, when children have a baguette sandwich and a glass of chocolate milk (*Cola Cao*). A popular sandwich filling is several pieces of chocolate.

Dinner

Spaniards eat in the evening from 9pm onwards (as late as 11pm in the summer) and dinner traditionally consists of a main course – some households have two courses – and dessert. Although dinner is lighter than the midday meal, it's invariably cooked and what the Spaniards call a 'proper meal' rather than a snack.

Bread

Bread is an essential part of a Spanish meal. In informal settings the bread is usually sliced into a basket, which is placed in the centre of the table and handed round as required. At a formal meal, bread rolls on small dishes or plates are placed to the left of each person.

You should break off a small piece of bread with your fingers and eat it whole rather than bite into a large piece, which is considered rude even at informal tables. If there's a knife with the bread, use this to spread the butter (if served, which is rare except in smart restaurants), not to cut the bread.

Bread is eaten as an accompaniment to other food and not on its own. Using it to mop up the remains of a sauce or soup is acceptable at an informal table – spear the bread with your fork rather than use your fingers – but you should never do this at a formal

> As is often the case, Spaniards' conceptions of other countries are often based on out-dated clichés: don't be surprised if guests ask you strange questions about your country, such as 'How do Londoners cope with the fog every day?' or 'Don't Americans get tired of eating hamburgers all the time?'

meal. You don't have to finish your bread or even eat any at all.

Conversation

What you talk about during a meal depends very much on the occasion and how well you know your host(s).

As a general rule, it's best to let the host lead the conversation and do most of the talking. Stick to neutral and impersonal topics such as the weather, local events and your holidays. Expect other guests to ask you questions about your home country and your impressions of Spain – keep to the positive ones. Avoid asking people personal questions unless you know them well and don't talk about work unless someone else raises the subject. It's polite to compliment your host on the meal.

Cutlery

Formal Dining

Cutlery (silverware) for the first and second courses will be arranged on the right and left sides of your place setting and you should work from the outside in, i.e. the outermost implements are for the first course.

Dessert cutlery is always placed above the place setting. Most food should be eaten using cutlery and you should always use both a knife and fork if they're provided. At very formal occasions you should eat all food without touching it, but if you're served something you would usually eat with your hands, e.g. langoustines or a banana, wait to see how the host eats it and follow suit – if the host uses his hands, it's appropriate for you to do so too.

When you've finished eating, you should place your knife and fork side by side in the middle of the plate.

Informal Dining

In informal settings, many Spaniards eat food with a fork only and use a piece of bread to push food onto the fork rather than a knife. It's also acceptable to eat some food with your fingers, e.g. shellfish or croquettes.

On the other hand, Spaniards eat most fruit using cutlery even on informal occasions. Fruit such as apples and pears is usually cut into pieces, not eaten off the core, and oranges are peeled using a knife and fork, not your fingers. Practise at home if you aren't used to this.

Grace

Some households say grace before a meal. If this is the case, you should sit with your head bowed until it's finished. Catholic guests say '*amén*' and cross themselves at the end of grace.

When to Start

It's polite to wait for everyone to be served (irrespective of the formality of the occasion) before starting a meal. At formal meals you should wait for the host to start before you do, unless he gives you permission to start first.

Noises

Coughing and blowing your nose loudly at the table are considered rude. If you need to cough, do it discreetly into your serviette and if you need to blow your nose, do so quietly. Burping is a no-no and should be avoided at all costs. If you cannot hold a loud noise in, say '*perdón*' quietly and act as if nothing has happened.

Seating

On formal occasions, guests are usually seated alternately male and

Don't expect a cheese sandwich and a flask of coffee on a Spanish picnic; whatever the location, tablecloths and serviettes adorn the ground and tables groan under platters of food. Chunks of tortilla, a variety of cold meats and salads, and empanada (tuna and tomato pastry) are usual picnic fare, together with a selection of desserts a generous quantities of wine and beer.

Smoking

Legislation introduced in January 2006 bans smoking in work places and most public areas, and restricts smoking in bars, restaurants and clubs. Those with premises larger than 100 m² are permitted to have up to 30 per cent of the space for smokers, but the allocated area must be completely enclosed and have its own ventilation system. Smoking in premises under 100 m² is permitted, but there must be a sign on the entrance clearly stating whether smoking is allowed. A recent study claimed that up to 90 per cent of premises under 100 m² have opted to allow smoking in order not to lose customers (most of whom smoke), with the result that small bars and cafés are now smokier than ever. Smoking is permitted in all outside terrace areas.

female, with the hosts at the ends of the table. It's polite to wait for the host to tell you where to sit and not to sit down until you're invited to do so. On big occasions such as weddings or banquets, cards with guests' names are placed on the tables. It's considered impolite to change places before or during a meal, but after dessert guests are free to mingle and sit elsewhere.

Table Manners

You should eat with both hands above the table, use your serviette often to wipe the corners of your mouth (and fingers) and keep your elbows off the table, although diners at informal meals often sit with both elbows on the table between courses.

Toasts

Toasts (*brindis*) aren't common in Spain. When appropriate, the host usually proposes a toast and guests raise their glasses and say '*¡Salud.*' ('Good health'). On informal occasions glasses are sometimes clinked.

DRINKING

Low taxes mean that Spain has the cheapest alcohol in the EU (e.g. a good bottle of wine can be had for €3 and a bottle of spirits for €6) and alcohol is part and parcel of everyday life. Many adults have a daily tipple and the drinking of wine and *cava* (Spanish sparkling wine) isn't limited to special occasions or Sunday lunches – a glass of *cava* is served as an aperitif in many restaurants in Catalonia. All bars and cafés serve alcohol, there are no licensing laws restricting hours of consumption and, although under 18s aren't permitted to buy alcohol, a blind eye is often turned.

Alcoholism and drunkenness aren't prevalent in Spain, although many towns and cities suffer the noise and litter caused by *botellón* – groups of

young people drinking in the squares and parks until the small hours. Most Spaniards drink in moderation and few go on 'binges' at weekends. Drunkenness is generally deplored – the Spaniards have an extremely low opinion of semi-conscious foreigners rampaging in resorts.

CAFES, BARS & RESTAURANTS

Spain offers a wealth of eateries, from luxury gourmet restaurants (with matching prices) to humble bars serving homely fare for a few euros.

Cafés & Bars

Café (and bar) culture is very strong in Spain and it isn't unusual to eat (and drink) out for breakfast, lunch and dinner. The selection and choice of food depends on the establishment, but most cafés offer hot and cold snacks such as *tapas* and sandwiches, and many serve meals at lunchtime and evenings. The following, sometimes surprising, facts apply to cafés and bars:

- **Alcohol** – All cafés and bars serve alcohol during opening hours. Bottled and cask beer, wine and spirits are available, but the

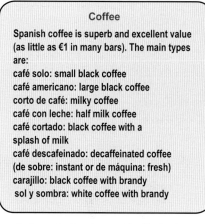

Coffee

Spanish coffee is superb and excellent value (as little as €1 in many bars). The main types are:
café solo: small black coffee
café americano: large black coffee
corto de café: milky coffee
café con leche: half milk coffee
café cortado: black coffee with a splash of milk
café descafeinado: decaffeinated coffee (de sobre: instant or de máquina: fresh)
carajillo: black coffee with brandy
sol y sombra: white coffee with brandy

choice of wine is usually limited to a house red and white.

- **Noise** – Enjoying a quiet coffee in a Spanish bar is often a challenge unless you sit outside and the tables aren't next to a busy road. Decibel levels in bars are invariably high: coffee grinders, milk heaters, 'singing' fruit machines, TVs at full volume (usually with no one watching) and clients all talking at once conspire to make having a coffee one of Spain's noisiest day-to-day experiences.

- **Opening hours** – Cafés usually open early in the morning and close late at night: 7am to midnight are typical hours. Those near public transport facilities such as mainline stations, on motorways and at airports usually open round the clock.

- **Ordering & paying** – Unless you're sitting at the bar (in which case you order directly from the staff behind the bar), you must wait for a waiter to come to your table to place your order. When you've finished, ask the waiter for the bill and pay him. Some more up-market cafés and those in tourist spots charge extra if you sit at a table or outside rather than at the bar, but in most bars and cafés the prices are the same irrespective of where you sit.

- **Service** – Waiter service is available at most cafés and there are very few self-service establishments in Spain.

- **Tips** – There's no standard tip and in a café or bar most people leave nothing or small change only. If you have a large bill and/or the service was particularly good, you might leave a few euros as a tip.

You may be surprised to see toothpicks (palillos de dientes) on a table, even in a formal setting. Some people, usually men, use one after a meal and it isn't considered rude to pick your teeth as long as you cover your mouth with your other hand while you do so.

restaurants close one day or evening a week, usually Sunday evening and possibly also the whole of Monday or Tuesday. Many close for holidays in January or August for at least two weeks. In seasonal resort areas, many restaurants (and bars) close for the whole of the winter.

- **Booking** – It's wise to book a table, particularly if you want to eat out on a Sunday or public holiday, when most of Spain goes out for lunch. Bookings can be made in person or by telephone. It's polite to telephone to cancel a booking if you cannot go.

- **Seating** – When you enter a restaurant, a waiter usually takes you to a table. If there are several free tables you may be offered a choice. Some restaurants have a sign at the entrance asking you to wait there for a waiter to show you in.

- **Table settings** – Depending on the type of restaurant, settings range from a knife and fork wrapped in a paper serviette to full silver service with linen napkins. A bread basket and possibly a plate of olives is usually brought to the table shortly after you sit down. Many restaurants now make a 'cover' charge (*pan y cubierto* – literally 'bread and cutlery'), usually stated in (very) small print at the

Restaurants

When eating out in Spain, bear in mind the following:

- **Opening hours** – Restaurants generally open from 1 or 1.30pm to 4pm for lunch and from 8.30 to 11pm for dinner. Those located in resort areas open earlier. Most end of the menu. This is generally from €0.50 to €2 per person and is added to bill irrespective of whether you eat the bread and olives or not.

- **Menu** – Most restaurants offer first courses (*primer plato* – soups, stews, salads, pasta), second courses (*segundo plato* – usually meat or fish) and desserts (*postre*). Most Spaniards have a first and second course, but coffee instead of a dessert. If you choose to have only one course while other people are having two, you can ask the waiter to bring your meal with their second course. It's acceptable to share first courses and desserts, but not second courses. Many restaurants offer children's menus or provide half (or smaller) portions for children under 12 if you ask.

- **Service** – Waiting is a profession in Spain, where there are few casual waiters (except in beach bars) and standards of service are usually high. Waiters should serve from the right and take from the left and never pass plates across the table. They should offer wine to be tasted before serving it, and plates should be cleared only when everyone has finished eating.If service is slow, it's acceptable to mention this to the waiter and ask politely for quicker service, but if the restaurant is very busy this may be impossible. Note also that in many restaurants food is cooked to order (rather than heated up) so you must wait at least 15 minutes for your first course. If a dish takes longer to prepare, e.g. a rice dish (paella cooked to order takes at least 30 minutes),

the waiter should inform you of this when you order.If a waiter is rude, it's best not to take this up with him directly but ask to see the head waiter (*maitre* or *camerero jefe*) or manager (*director*). If your complaints aren't resolved satisfactorily, ask for the complaints book (*libro de reclamaciones*) and make your complaint in writing. In most cases, merely asking for the complaints book improves service no end.

- **Water** – If you don't want to pay for mineral water, ask for *agua del grifo* (tap water) or *una jarra de agua* (a jug of water). Some good restaurants provide mineral water free of charge.

Many eateries offer a 'menu of the day' (menú del día) consisting of two main courses (there's usually a choice of several dishes for each course) and dessert or coffee plus bread and a drink. Food is generally home cooked, of high quality and excellent value – expect to pay from €6 to €10 per person. To find the best food, look for crowded bars and restaurants at 2pm.

- **The bill** – When you're ready for the bill, you should attract the waiter's attention by catching his eye, waving him over or calling '*oiga*' (literally 'listen'). To ask for the bill you should say '*La cuenta, por favor.*' Few waiters bring you the bill unprompted.

- **Tipping** – There's no statutory amount that should be left as a tip and the amount you leave is an indication of how good you thought the food and service was. If you've enjoyed your meal and received good service, leave between 5 and 10 per cent of the bill. It isn't usual practice to add the tip to your credit card payment and bills don't include an amount you fill in as a tip. Tips must be left as cash.

> Most bakeries in Spain make birthday cakes (tarta de cumpleaños) to order and prices are usually reasonable. Designs are varied and can be customised. Cakes usually consist of several layers of sponge with a creamy filling, sometimes in different flavours, and topped with cream.

NIGHTLIFE

The Spanish are night owls – Madrileños are known nationally as cats (*gatos*) because of their nocturnal hours – and the country is famous for its vibrant nightlife. In major cities and resort areas, there's a wide choice of nightlife for all ages, including jazz clubs, cabarets, discos, sex shows, flamenco clubs and night clubs (known as *pubs* in Spanish but bearing no relation to pubs in the UK). Even the smallest

Festival Las Fallas, Valencia

self-respecting town has at least one disco where you can dance the night away until dawn.

Before you sample the Spanish club scene, note the following:

- **Opening hours** – Few nightlife venues open before 10pm and many don't open until midnight. Those in remote areas (i.e. where there aren't any neighbours to complain) stay open until dawn – Ibiza has 24-hour nightclubs – but nightclubs in urban areas must close by 4.30am.

- **Age** – You must usually be at least 18 and you may be asked for proof of your age before being let in. Some nightclubs have 'early' evening sessions, e.g. from 9 to 11pm, for teenagers.

- **Dress code** – Casual dress is the norm for most nightclubs, although some don't allow jeans. Women can usually get away with any outfit and in some venues scantily dressed women get in free. See also **Bouncers** below.

- **Bouncers** – Nightclub bouncers (many of them security guards earning extra money in their time off) have a formidable reputation in Spain as they like to throw their weight around (literally). Bouncers, 99.9 per cent of whom are men, tend to be stricter with male party-goers and getting into a nightclub sometimes depends on whether the bouncer likes the look of you; if they don't like your trainers or T-shirt they may refuse you entry. If a bouncer refuses you entry, it's best not to argue (particularly if you're a man) and go elsewhere.

- **Drinks** – Clubs serve all types of alcoholic and non-alcoholic drinks with the exception of hot drinks – few venues serve coffee. Entrance fees (usually from €5) sometimes include a drink; some clubs have no entrance fee and drinks cost from €3 to over €20, depending on the establishment. Cocktails cost at least €8.

- **Buying rounds & paying** – In most clubs you order at the bar and pay when your drinks are served. In venues where there's waiter service, you pay when the waiter brings a round of drinks

> Spain is the world record holder for the number of bars and restaurants per person – 1 for every 135 inhabitants.

rather than ask for the bill later.

FAMILY OCCASIONS

Family occasions form an important part of the Spanish social calendar and are usually large, loud gatherings giving the host(s) an ideal opportunity to 'shine' in front of others. The most important family gatherings are as follows.

Birthdays

Birthdays are low-key occasions and some Spaniards mark their saint's day (e.g. San José on 19th March for anyone called José) rather than their birthday. Birthday cards aren't usually sent and presents are generally small. 'Landmark' birthdays, e.g. 40 and 50, aren't particularly special and there are no expressions in Spanish referring to specific ages, such as 'life begins at 40'. If it's your birthday and you go out with others for drinks, you pay.

Small children usually have birthday parties and these are often held at play parks or fast food restaurants such as McDonald's. It's common to invite lots of friends – the whole school class isn't unusual – and children's birthday parties can be costly events.

Christenings

The vast majority of Spanish children are baptized at a Catholic ceremony and christenings (*bautizo*) are important social occasions – there may be up to a hundred guests – but are considerably less formal than weddings. Children are baptized young – at around three months – and have one godfather (*padrino*) and one godmother (*madrina*), both of whom are usually close family members. If you're asked to be a godparent of a Spanish child, take this as a great honour and privilege. Duties include bringing up the child in the Catholic (or other) faith, helping with the child's upbringing, giving generous birthday and Christmas presents, and assuming guardianship should the parents die.

The church ceremony is followed by a large meal, usually at a restaurant rather than the parents' home. Dress is smart-casual – godparents dress more formally – and you should take a gift for the child.

Engagement Parties

Once a couple has announced their intention to marry, it's traditional to have an engagement party (*pedida* – literally, 'petition'). This custom is dying out, but many families still observe it. The party is held in the future bride's home and the only guests are the groom-to-be's family and possibly close friends. The groom (or sometimes his parents) asks for the bride's hand and presents her with an engagement ring, which she wears on her left ring finger (wedding rings

are usually worn on the right ring finger). The bride and her parents accept the marriage petition and offer the groom a present, usually a watch. Once the *pedida* is over, the date for the wedding is set. This is a reasonably formal occasion, although dress is smart-casual, and provides a chance for the two families to meet and break the ice before the wedding.

First Communions

Although many Spaniards are ambivalent about religion and only around 20 per cent of the population attend mass regularly, the vast majority of Spanish children take their First Holy Communion between the ages of 8 and 10, and the accompanying celebrations are a major social event, on which families spend an average of €2,500 per child.

Most first communions take place on Saturdays in spring and involve complex logistics. First communion girls are dressed in long, white dresses with matching shoes, hair accessories, gloves and possibly flowers, and boys wear navy sailor suits or black suits. After the church service, usually in the morning, guests (at least 30) are treated to lunch in a nearby restaurant. Formal photographs are taken of the child – the best takes pride of place in the parents' home for ever afterwards – who has almost God-like status throughout the day.

Dress is smart-casual, although the parents usually dress very smartly and you're expected to take a gift for the child. First communion presents are often large and expensive – the pile of gifts on show at the restaurant would be the envy of any toy shop – and you should spend at least €30, more if you're a close friend. Guests are presented with a small gift or card at the end of the celebrations to commemorate the occasion.

Christmas & New Year

Spaniards' main Christmas celebration is held on Christmas Eve (24th December), when it's traditional for the whole family

> A dozen grapes are served at midnight and these are eaten from the first stroke of the clock, the idea being to eat them all before the clock finishes striking out the old year. Each grape represents a month of luck for the coming year so the more you manage to eat, the better your year will be.

to gather for dinner. The meal starts late (around 10pm) and lasts well into the small hours. Food is usually rich and 'luxury' – typical fare includes langoustines, lobster, shellfish, roast lamb and suckling pig – and there are several courses. Wine and *cava* are drunk. Dessert is usually a huge platter of sweetmeats such as marzipan, chocolates and *turrón* (almond sweets, similar to nougat). Some families exchange presents at this time, although traditionally Christmas gifts are given on 6th January (see below).

Christmas decorations tend to be low-key in Spain, although in recent years people have started decorating their balconies with flashing lights and climbing Santas, but relatively few households put up a tree. Most households set up a nativity scene (*belén*), which is often a work of art with miniature figures, houses and scenery representing the Christmas story. The best have night and day lighting, working parts and piped music. Most towns have a large municipal *belén*.

Christmas carols (*villancicos*) are noisy affairs – forget peaceful choirs – with groups of singers playing drums and tambourines and scraping glass bottles with sticks (the 'cut glass' of an *anís* liqueur bottle makes the best noise). In Andalusia, groups of Christmas carol singers known as *pastorales* dress up as shepherds and sing in town centres.

New Year's Eve is also very much a family affair in Spain, where it's traditional for the whole family to have dinner together before midnight – celebrations with friends take place after midnight. Food is similar to that eaten on Christmas Eve.

Epiphany

Father Christmas or Santa Claus does visit Spain, but not all households – he's very much a foreign import and his presence isn't as strong as that of the Three Wise Men or Three Kings (*reyes magos*), who are the traditional bearers of presents in Spain. Most towns and cities have carnival-like parades during late afternoon and early evening of 5th January in which the Kings are represented. The parades are often spectacular – in coastal towns, the Kings may arrive by boat; elsewhere they may ride camels – and some, such as those in Madrid and Barcelona, have numerous floats and live music. Thousands of kilos of sweets are thrown to the watching children and their families.

After the parade, children put their shoes outside their bedroom door and wake up to find their presents on the morning of 6th January (Epiphany), a national holiday. Children who have been naughty during the year receive coal (*carbón*) instead of presents and many bakeries sell 'coal' made out of blown sugar for the occasion.

> September is the most popular month for weddings, followed by May and June. Most couples get married on a Saturday.

Weddings

Weddings are the social event *par excellence* in any Spaniard's calendar and tend to be bigger and brighter than those in many other European countries – Spaniards spend a small fortune (between €20,000 and €35,000) on the occasion, so if you're invited to a wedding you can expect a proper celebration. There are usually at least 100 guests – many weddings have 200 upwards – and the festivities last hours and always well into the early morning.

Invitations

Formal invitations are usually sent by post a couple of months before the event. Invitations to church weddings include the letters *D.M.* after the time, e.g. '*a las cinco de la tarde, D.M.*', which stand for *Dios mediante*, meaning 'in God's presence'. Both sets of parents invite guests (costs are usually shared), but you reply to one only, usually the one you know. Replies should be in writing or by telephone and it's polite to reply at least two weeks before the event.

1st November

All Saints' Day or All Souls' Day (día de todos los santos) is a national holiday in Spain and traditionally the time of year when Spaniards honour their dead and visit their burial places. Cemeteries are a hive of activity for most of the day as relatives scrub and clean graves, and lay fresh flowers.

Gifts

Wedding etiquette dictates that your gift to the happy couple should cost at least as much as the meal you're treated to. Given that most meals are luxury, three-course affairs, you should spend at least €40 on a gift – double that if two of you are going. Most couples have a wedding present list (*lista de bodas*) and the invitation often includes this or tells you where the chosen items can be bought – needless to say, El Corte Inglés is the most popular spot for wedding present lists. The procedure for buying present is easy if impersonal: you go to customer services, give the names of the couple and receive a (usually very long) printed list of gift requests. These range from toilet roll holders to plasma TVs costing thousands of euros. More expensive gifts are usually divided into 'lots' so you can, for example, buy the couple a sixth of a fridge or a quarter of a mattress. You pay for the gift, which is then allocated your name on the list, but you don't take it away with you.

Some guests prefer to buy something more personal and take it to the wedding. In some parts of Spain, particularly provincial towns, it's customary to give the couple an envelope containing money. In this case, you should give at least €100.

If you know the couple reasonably well and cannot go to the wedding, you're expected to buy a gift.

Dress

Spaniards tend to dress extremely smartly for weddings and the most important people (see **Key Players** below) dress lavishly in outfits costing hundreds of euros.

Important men are expected to wear morning suits (usually black), but not hats, and important women wear cocktail dresses with sumptuous matching accessories; many wear the traditional black lace mantilla.

Hats are acceptable for midday weddings, although few women wear them. A visit to the hairdresser is *de rigueur* for female guests, all of whom will be highly made up.

Bear in mind that it's worth making an effort and dressing up too, as your outfit and appearance will be amply commented on in the wedding *post mortem*.

Key Players

Apart from the bride and groom, the following people are important at Spanish weddings:

- **Bride's father** (*padrino*) – accompanies the bride down the aisle;
- **Groom's mother** (*madrina*) – accompanies the groom down the aisle;
- **Bridesmaids & pages** (*damas de honor* & *pajes*) – accompany

the bride down the aisle, usually in front. They tend to be young children, the eldest carrying the rings and coins (see **Procedure**).

- **Witnesses** (chosen beforehand and known as *testigos*) – when the vows have been exchanged, close friends and relatives witness the marriage by signing the certificate.

Procedure

The vast majority of weddings are held in the late afternoon and evening; the ceremony is typically at 5 or 6pm. Church ceremonies include mass, communion (guests may take part), a sermon, the wedding vows and the witnessing.

Live music is sometimes included, although this isn't common. Expect the ceremony to last around 40 minutes, although some last longer. Civil wedding ceremonies – these take place in town and city halls (*ayuntamiento*) – last around 15 to 20 minutes and include the wedding vows and perhaps a short speech by the mayor or his substitute. At all ceremonies, the couple exchange rings and 13 small coins (*arras*), symbolising the wealth they will share.

When the couple come out of the church or town hall, guests shower them with rice (uncooked) and shout '*vivan los novios*' ('long live the couple'). Everyone then kisses and congratulates the couple before they're whisked off for extensive photo sessions, usually in a 'romantic' location such as a park or beach. The photo shoot often lasts at least an hour, during which time guests are expected to amuse themselves before the celebrations start. Don't be surprised if you have a couple of hours to kill before the meal, which usually starts at 9pm.

Food and drink flow at Spanish weddings: aperitifs are served when guests arrive and there's usually a formal three-course meal with wine. Dessert is always the wedding cake – this consists of several (at least five) tiers of sponge cake decorated with cream and crowned with a miniature bride and groom. There are no formal speeches and a general toast is made when the couple cut the cake.

After the meal, there's live music and dancing – the bride and groom start proceedings with a waltz and then the bride waltzes with her father and the groom with his mother. Dancing continues for several hours and thirsts are quenched with drinks from the bar (usually free). It's common for guests, particularly younger ones, to continue well into the morning, and at some weddings hot chocolate and *churros* (thick fried dough sticks) are served to survivors at around 4am.

Funerals

Funerals are multitudinous affairs in Spain, where news of a death travels fast and most locals pay their respects to the family before the burial or cremation, even if they don't know them well. In small towns and villages, coffins are usually laid in the family home; elsewhere they are put in a purpose-built municipal morgue (*tanatorio*), usually near or within the burial ground and complete with a chapel and crematorium (and bar).

> The Spanish bury or cremate their dead the day after death, which means it can be difficult to get to a funeral. However, if you cannot make it, you can go to the memorial service (funeral), usually held a week later.

Coffins may be displayed closed or open – those close to the deceased may kiss the body and some mourners lay a flower, usually a red or white carnation, on the coffin. Families are allocated a private room for the wake (*velatorio*), which lasts until burial (*entierro*) or cremation (*incineración*) the following day. Grief is sometimes expressed openly, with loud sobbing or even wailing.

To pay your respects you should approach the family (widow or widower first), shake hands with or kiss them and say '*le acompaño en los sentimientos*' ('I share your grief'). Only close family and friends send flowers – large and

often elaborate wreaths. The family offers no food or drink after the burial.

Cremation isn't popular in Spain and most Spaniards are interred in 'niches' (*nichos*) arranged in tiers – not unlike an apartment block – around the cemetery. The deceased's family rents a niche for a number of years (e.g. five, although a rental can be renewed), after which time the body is moved to common burial ground.

Dress

Many mourners wear black to a funeral or memorial service, although this is no longer obligatory and any sombre colours are acceptable. In rural areas, widows and their daughters wear black for at least a year after their husband's/ father's death, but this tradition is gradually dying out.

CLUBS

Social and sports clubs exist throughout Spain and joining a club is an excellent way to meet people and make friends. Most local councils offer a variety of clubs in their municipality and most towns have social centres for retirees (*hogar del pensionista*). Clubs are also organised by national and international associations (e.g. political parties and Rotary International), sports centres and groups of individuals.

You must usually pay a membership fee – clubs run by councils are subsidised for local residents – and you may have to be recommended by two other members in order to join. Associations in Spain are governed by strict regulations (no one escapes the paperwork): they must publish a list of statutes and hold elections and an annual general meeting, of which detailed minutes must be taken. If you join an association – even if it's a local football team – don't be surprised if you receive a long list of your 'rights and obligations' (*derechos y deberes*) as a member.

How strictly these are adhered to depends on the club, but some follow them to the letter.

Brotherhoods

Brotherhoods (*cofradías* or *hermandades*) form an essential part of Catholic life in Spain, where there are hundreds of brotherhoods, each representing a particular church or saint or virgin, e.g. Hermandad de la Virgen del Rocío. They're particularly common in the south of Spain – Seville holds the record – but can be found in most towns and cities.

A brotherhood's main purpose is religious instruction, and prayers and all-night vigils form an essential part of membership, but brotherhoods also carry out social and charitable acts such as visiting the old and sick, and raising money for a local cause. Requirements for membership are usually strict – some admit only highly recommended community figures – and for most you need to 'prove' your religious background and beliefs. Annual subscriptions and donations are also usually essential.

Brotherhoods are most visible during Holy Week and on other important religious occasions, when they're in charge of the procession – members decorate and carry or parade alongside a float.

Sociedades Gastronómicas

In a country where advances in the quest for sexual equality are almost a daily occurrence, it's surprising to find that all-male dining clubs, known as *sociedades gastronómicas* (*txokos* in Basque), are alive and well – at least in the north of Spain, particularly in the Basque Country.

The first club was founded in San Sebastián in the mid-19th century and there are now several dozen. Their main objective is to promote local food and wine, and to this end they organise regular meals. Women are permitted to attend only if they're invited by a male member (some clubs don't allow women to weekend meetings) and women guests are never allowed to cook – a measure they would welcome in their homes.

On the night of 19th January, the dining clubs of San Sebastián celebrate their annual dinner, after which half the members dress up as chefs (some carry giant spoons) and the other half as soldiers in Napoleonic costume and they parade through the local streets beating drums and wooden buckets (*tamborrada*).

POPULAR CULTURE

Although Spaniards have a strong sense of individuality, they like to do things *en masse*. This is particularly apparent at the beach in summer or in the countryside in winter, when many Spanish family groups, consisting of at least ten adults plus children, set up mini-campsites with awnings, chairs, tables, sun-loungers and a barbecue; televisions and even drinks trolleys complete with whisky decanter and glasses have been seen.

In times of national mourning or political tension, on the other hand, Spaniards of all ages demonstrate on the streets in their thousands – or millions, as when protesters lined

Spain's avenues after the Islamist bomb attacks on Madrid trains in March 2004. A year earlier record numbers marched against military intervention in Iraq – uplifting events that show the extent of Spanish social solidarity.

The feeling that individuals belong to a solid social network is inculcated from an early age: children are encouraged to take part in plenty of group activities, school trips are often organised (many residential) and it's common for them to go to camp for two weeks during the summer holidays.

Adolescents form large groups of friends known as *pandillas*, who go out together. Family units include both sets of grandparents and a seemingly endless succession of cousins, aunts and uncles – all cousins are called *primos*, even if they're third or fourth cousins.

Bullfighting

A book about Spanish culture wouldn't be complete without a section on bullfighting (*la lidia*), commonly referred to as the *fiesta nacional*. Bullfighting provokes controversy even among Spaniards. To many it's a barbaric and sadistic blood sport with no merit whatsoever and should be banned. It's claimed by those opposed to bullfighting that over 80 per cent of Spaniards are against it, although in fact most are probably indifferent. And the fact remains that bullfighting is highly popular, with over 40m paying spectators a year. Top fights are shown live on television and bullfighting is a major industry, moving millions of euros a year. On the other hand, it's banned in the Canary Islands and in a few areas in mainland Spain, including Barcelona, which joined the anti-bullfighting league in 2004 – much to the surprise of many Spaniards.

Bullfighting isn't considered a sport by aficionados, but an art, and it's reported in the arts and culture section of newspapers. It certainly isn't a contest, as there can be only one 'winner', although bullfighters get killed every year (in addition to some 8,000 bulls and a few spectators who jump into the ring to try their luck). Fans hail it as a spectacle encompassing colour, tradition, excitement, pageantry, beauty, danger, bravery, skill, suffering and drama. Love it or loathe it, bullfighting is an essential

> If you decide to go to a bullfight, you should never cheer for the bull, particularly if it has gored the bullfighter (matador or torero), unless you wish to be the object of hostility from the crowd.

Running of the bulls, Pamplona

TV off and it won't have cost you anything.

Festivals & Fairs

Festivals (*fiestas*) and fairs (*ferias*) form an essential part of cultural and social life in Spain, where even the smallest village holds at least one big party a year. Spanish festivals are colourful events, usually noisy with loud music and plenty of fireworks – expect to see world class displays at most places – and lasting several days, during which the locality comes almost to a standstill.

Essential ingredients include processions (often religious), music, dancing and feasting (including large quantities of alcohol).

Festivals in some areas also include bulls – bull-running and bullfighting. Everyone can join in, foreigners included, and there's rarely any violence or serious crime, although pickpockets and bag snatchers are fairly common at the biggest events.

Spain's largest festivals are as follows (in chronological order):

- **Carnival** – held in February, around Mardi Gras, and celebrated throughout Spain. The most famous celebrations are in Gran Canaria and Tenerife, where the festivities are similar to those in Rio de Janeiro, and in Cadiz.
- **Holy Week** – the most important event in the religious calendar, when solemn religious processions are held throughout Spain, although those in Andalusia are particularly famous. The mostly silent processions consist of women

part of Spain's heritage and culture and, perhaps more than anything else, is emblematic of the Spanish obsession with living intensely (and recklessly) because death may be just round the corner.

If you're opposed to bullfighting, it's best not to go to a fight, as you certainly won't enjoy it and may well be distressed. If you feel you ought to watch it at least once, it's advisable to watch a fight on TV before deciding whether to see one 'in the flesh'. Not only do you see a lot of blood but bullfights are long (five bulls are usually killed) and can be tedious – at least you can turn the

There are no vociferous national movements against hunting; public opinion is temporarily outraged if a bear or lynx is killed, but the fact that thousands of animals are shot annually doesn't cause national concern. Most Spaniards are indifferent to game sports and many feel they're part and parcel of everyday life. Avoid voicing strong opposition to hunting or fishing unless you're with Spaniards who you know will be sympathetic.

dressed in black (often barefoot in penance) carrying candles, and huge, ornate floats weighing several tonnes and depicting scenes from the Passion. The floats are carried on the shoulders of around 50 men, who march for short distances at a time before resting. Also accompanying the procession are the penitents (*penitentes*) dressed in purple or black robes and pointed hats with masks. Occasional mournful music is provided by municipal brass bands (the standard of playing varies considerably, but keep your expectations low to avoid disappointment).

Processions last several hours and it's often late at night before each float returns to its church.

In Andalusia, spontaneous *saetas* (flamenco laments) are often sung in homage to the float as it passes – the combination of the candle-lit procession and the deep laments is often a spine-tingling experience.

- **San José** – Valencia offers one of Spain's most colourful (and loudest) celebrations in honour

> The penitents' conical hats and masks were imitated by the Ku Klux Klan in the US, but in Spain the outfit has profoundly religious significance rather than anything to do with racial discrimination.

of San José (St Joseph). Huge papier-mâché effigies are erected around the city and burnt on the night of 19th March amid huge celebrations and tonnes of fireworks.

- **San Juan** – Many Mediterranean towns and villages hold all-night parties on the night of 22nd June in honour of San Juan (St John) and celebrating the arrival of summer. Bonfires are lit on beaches – rituals include leaping through fire and/or bathing in the sea at midnight as a means of purification, and taking sea water home to sprinkle in the four corners of every room to keep evil spirits away.

- **Virgen del Carmen** – Most coastal towns and villages celebrate the patron of fishermen's day on 16th July, when the Virgin's image is paraded in boats along the coast.

Local festivals are usually celebrated on the local saint's day or mark a significant local event, e.g. a wine harvest or deliverance from the Moors. Torremolinos on the Costa del Sol even celebrates its tourists with an annual 'Tourism Day', held in early June.

Gambling

Luck and chance (*suerte* and *azar*) play an important part in Spanish culture and the Spaniards rely heavily on things turning out all right in the end – the expression '*ojalá*' ('here's hoping…') is used frequently in conversation. It therefore perhaps isn't surprising that they're a nation of gamblers, and bet a higher proportion of their income than almost any other nation, with an annual national average of over €200 per person.

The most popular forms of gambling are lotteries (*lotería*) and the football pools (*quiniela*). Slot machines and bingo are also popular, but betting shops such as those found in the UK are illegal and only exist 'secretly' in some resort areas.

The state national lottery (*lotería nacional*) is the most popular lottery – despite the fact that tickets cost a whopping €20 from official lottery outlets or €22 from street vendors – and offers the world's largest prize, appropriately known as the 'Fat One' (*El Gordo*), held on 22nd December. National lottery draws are held on Saturdays and televised live – winning numbers are 'sung' by children from the San Ildefonso boarding school in Madrid.

The Spanish organisation for the blind and disabled, ONCE, also sells lottery tickets from kiosks manned by employees with disabilities.

There's a daily draw (Friday has the largest prize – €6m), *combo* cards (a combination of six numbers placed in a triangle), and scratch cards (known as *Rasca y Gana*). ONCE takes some €60 a year from every Spaniard and has a massive turnover that many companies would be proud of.

> A staggering 57 per cent of Spaniards buy a ticket for 'El Gordo', the Christmas lottery, seemingly undeterred by the unlikelihood of winning the top prize – one in 14.5m.

Street Life

It's often said that Spaniards 'live' on the street rather than in their homes and a common social activity in the early evening is to go out for a stroll, not so much for the exercise but to see and be seen – '*ir a la calle*' ('taking to the streets') is a well used phrase. Spanish town and city streets are packed by 7pm (9pm in the summer, once it cools down). Cafés are popular venues, as they provide a good vantage point for people-watching, and a drink can last at least an hour. Benches are well used – Spanish towns have dozens of benches lining the streets – and their occupants watch the world go by for hours on end. In villages, it's common for people to take chairs out on to the streets as a means of participating in this collective activity.

Pipas (unshelled sunflower seeds) are part and parcel of the 'taking to the streets' experience and every self-respecting Spaniard is a master in the art of shelling a sunflower seed with his front teeth, eating the seed and spitting out the shell – all in the space of a second. Benches surrounded by hundreds of sunflower seed shells are a common sight. The phrase 'Tienes pipas?' ('Got any sunflower seeds?'), however, means your fly is undone.

Spectator Sports

Watching sport is a national pastime but it's dominated by football, other sports taking very much a back seat. Sports newspapers (around 75 per cent of them dedicated to football) are the most-read dailies.

Football

Spanish football fans are among the most dedicated and fervent in Europe, perhaps matched in their fanaticism only by the Italians.

During and after matches every move is discussed and analysed, and Spanish fans are so knowledgeable about the game that they almost

always know better than the coach, manager and referee… This is particularly true if the national team is playing, when it's supported by 44m 'coaches' and 'managers'.

Football games are major televised events, particularly important league games and UEFA Champions Leagues matches. World and European cups are even more 'important' and few things bring Spaniards together more than the Spanish football team's progress (or, usually, lack of progress) on the international football stage. During major football matches most of the country comes to a standstill – which is a good time to do some shopping or go to the beach. Even public life is affected – in April 2006, government proposals weren't ratified by the Senate because numerous senators in favour of them were reportedly watching Barcelona play Milan in the UEFA Cup.

Countless TV minutes are devoted to analysing every move made and every word uttered by football players and managers; all news bulletins include an item on football and the 'sports' section in most newspapers is devoted almost entirely to football. Only when Spaniards achieve international prowess in a sport other than football – such as winning the Formula One World Championship or the Basketball World Cup – is football (briefly) sidelined.

Football players are media stars and national icons, but the obsessive interest in them is mainly confined to the sport itself rather than their private lives – Raul's wife and children rarely make a news item and even Beckham's entourage sparks little interest. Ronaldinho's mother and brother made a brief appearance in a TV advert for custard in 2006, but otherwise the Brazilian's private life is out of the public eye.

Hooliganism and violence at football matches is relatively rare and most matches take place in an almost family atmosphere. The only incidents tend to occur at 'high-risk' matches such as those between Barça and Real Madrid, among whose fans are an extreme group known as the '*Ultras*'.

Football is **the** topic of conversation among many Spaniards – talk in bars, shops and on the street after a major match is about nothing else – and the following essential information should help you join in.

Real Madrid v Barcelona FC: Spain is home to some of the world's top football clubs, but Real Madrid and Barcelona (Barça) stand head and shoulders above the rest and have a huge international following – both clubs' websites have Japanese-language options and the teams spend August playing exhibition matches around the world. Real Madrid play at the imposing 130,000-seat Santiago Bernabeu stadium, while Barcelona's home is the equally impressive 120,000-seat Nou Camp stadium. Most Spaniards support either Real Madrid or Barcelona FC as well as their local team, and the twice-yearly league matches between the two teams are national events and commented on for weeks before and after the event.

Real Madrid has an impressive track record, boasting nine European Cups, two UEFA Cups and three Intercontinental Cups as well as being 29-times winner of the league. The club was home to the so-called Galactic team, which in its heyday in 2003/4 included several of the world's top players – Beckham, Figo, Raúl, Ronaldo and Zidane.

Barça also has a worthy collection of cups to its name, having won the Spanish league in the 2004/5 and 2005/6 seasons and the Champions League in 2006.

Spanish league: League (*liga*) matches take place from September to May on Wednesdays and at weekends (mostly on Sundays). There are three divisions: the first division (*primera división*) with 20 clubs, the bottom three going down into the second division at the end of each season; the second division

Real Madrid fans are known as los blancos (the whites) and los merengues (meringues) and Barça fans as los azulgrana (after their blue and maroon strips).

Major Sporting Events

The following annual sporting events are the most important in the Spanish calendar:

Canoeing – descent of the Sella River, from Arriondas to Ribadesella, Asturias (first Saturday in August);

Cycling – Vuelta de España, throughout the country (three weeks during September and October);

Football – the match that decides the league winners (usually in March); final of the Copa del Rey (towards the end of June); Real Madrid versus Barcelona FC (twice a year between September and May);

Formula One motorcycling – Spanish championships, Barcelona, Jerez and Valencia (Cheste);

Formula One motor racing – Spanish championship, Barcelona (May);

Golf – Volvo Masters, Valderrama, Costa del Sol (end of October);

Tennis – ATP Masters Series, Madrid

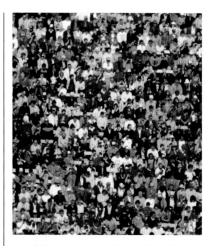

conditions – is that the influx of foreign stars into the first division makes it difficult for promising young Spanish players to get the necessary experience. Needless to say, most Spaniards have **the** solution to the national team's problems and these are discussed vociferously and endlessly in bars and shops.

Other Sports

Other sports pale in comparison with football, but many are nevertheless popular – especially the following:

Basketball: The national basketball league (*Liga ACB*, which stands for *Asociación de Clubs de Baloncesto*) is world class and thousands of fans follow their team's progress closely. Top teams include Real Madrid, Unicaja (from Malaga and 2005/6 league champions) and TAU Cerámica (from Vitoria). The national team won the World Championships in 2006 and several Spanish players compete in the NBA series in the US.

(*segunda división*) with 22 clubs; and the second division B (*segunda división B*) where there are four groups of 20 clubs each. All matches are televised but many are shown only on subscription channels. Local matches are shown on regional TV (e.g. Canal Sur in Andalusia) or local TV (e.g. Localia). Important matches are watched by millions and top audience ratings.

National team: Spain's national team, known as *La Selección*, is a constant source of disappointment to its millions of loyal fans – Spain only won one game in the 2004 European Cup and failed to reach the quarter-finals in the 2006 World Cup. One of the main problems – apart from a useless coach, biased refereeing and adverse weather

Most basketball teams are named after their sponsors rather than their hometown, e.g. Caja San Fernando (Seville) and DKV Joventut (Badalona in Catalonia).

Cycling: The Tour de France (which occasionally has stages in Spain) and the Vuelta de España (held over three weeks in September) are major spectator sports and followed by millions daily.

Motor racing & motorcycling: Both are increasingly popular spectator sports, particularly since the emergence of Fernando Alonso (Formula One world champion in 2005 and 2006) and leading motorcycle riders such as Dani Pedrosa, Jorge Lorenzo and Alvaro Bautista, all champions in their categories.

Tennis: Spain is one of the world's strongest tennis countries. Rafael Nadal is currently the country's top player and other key players include Feliciano López and Tommy Robledo – their fortunes closely followed.

Fans of sports that aren't popular in Spain (e.g. cricket and rugby) will be disappointed – satellite TV is a must if you want to watch the Ashes or the Six Nations' Cup. However, when Spain is taking part, sporting events (however obscure) are televised and given huge publicity.

Hunting & Fishing

So-called game sports are popular in Spain, where some of the world's best hunting (*caza*) and fishing (*pesca*) grounds can be found. Hunting isn't an elite sport, although traditionally it was practised by landowners, whose servants would fetch and carry game. The Spanish kill thousands of songbirds (*pajaritos*) each year, which are considered a delicacy by many people and are a favourite dish at the Seville Fair, as these are unprotected. Other popular game includes wild boar, hare, deer and wild goat.

Hunting takes place in many parts of the Spanish countryside including public land. Authorised hunting areas are marked by signs saying '*coto de caza*'. Take extra care when walking in an area where hunting is allowed. There's no tradition of conservation in Spain and most hunters are inclined to shoot anything that moves, including passers-by and each other – several people are killed every year in hunting accidents.

The hunting season varies according to the region and the game but generally lasts from October to early February.

Fishing is extremely popular in most parts of Spain and, as in many countries, an almost all-male pastime. Most anglers who fish from the beach or at sea take their catch home for lunch, but fish caught in reservoirs are usually thrown back in.

Museo del Prado, Madrid

THE ARTS

The arts aren't considered high-brow in Spain, where classical music, theatre and visual arts are almost as popular as the cinema and other forms of entertainment.

Booking

Tickets for 'cultural' events can be bought in the following ways:

- **At ATMs** – At Servicaixa ATMs (found in at least one La Caixa bank branch in most towns) you can book for many events and museums throughout Spain with any credit card. Booking is straightforward and you can usually choose your seat. Your tickets are printed immediately.

- **In person** – Many venues have yet to offer online and telephone booking (see below), so your only option is to go in person – no one books by post owing to the unreliability of the postal service. Depending on the popularity of an event, you may need to go early and queue for hours.

- **Online & by telephone** – Most large museums and theatres and almost all cinemas allow online and telephone booking, though few staff speak English and few websites offer an English-language option. Phone booking lines are often busy and it can be difficult to get through – early morning and lunchtime are the quietest times. Payment is via credit or debit card (check that the payment page starts 'https://') and there's often a booking fee of between €0.50 and €3. You cannot usually buy more than five or six tickets and these aren't sent to you. You should therefore arrive 30 minutes before the entry or start time to collect them – and you must usually show identification and the card you used to pay for the tickets.

In appreciation of a good performance, the Spanish shout 'bravo', start a prolonged handclap and may stamp their feet and shout either 'otro' or 'bis' ('encore').

Cinema & Theatre

When going to see a film or a play in Spain, bear in mind the following:

- **Disabled access** – Large cinema complexes have disabled access and many have disabled 'seats', a facility that isn't available in many theatres.

> The Museo del Prado (Madrid) receives nearly 2m visitors a year, the Reina Sofía (Madrid) 1.6m and the Guggenheim (Bilbao) around 1m.

- **Late arrivals** – If you arrive late for a theatre or concert performance, you'll have to wait for the interval or the end of the first act before you're allowed in. Entrance to a cinema is allowed at any time.

- **Noise** – Theatre-goers are usually quiet, but at cinemas many people chat through trailers and adverts, and some give a running commentary of events throughout the film itself. Mobile phones sometimes go off during a film and some people answer and have a conversation. Late arrivals rarely sit down quietly and adolescents and children's party groups also add to noise levels. If noise affects your enjoyment of a film, complain to the usher (*acomodador*).

- **Air-conditioning** – In the summer, most venues have the air-conditioning on high and can be freezing. Avoid wearing scanty clothes and take a sweater.

- **Food** – Theatre-goers rarely take food into the auditorium and at some theatres it's prohibited. Going to the cinema in Spain was until quite recently also a foodless experience, but nowadays, as in many other European countries, seeing a film is an opportunity to consume vast quantities of food and drink. Popcorn and soft drinks (both sold mostly in buckets) are standard cinema fare, along with sweets, chocolate and hotdogs.

Museums & Art Galleries

Spain has several world-class museums and art galleries housing unique treasures – those on show in the Prado, Thyssen Museum and Archeology Museum in Madrid are exceptional. Most cities and many towns have an art museum, often housing surprisingly famous paintings. The Spanish are proud of their national heritage (*patrimonio nacional*) and museums are popular. Schools frequently organise class trips to museums so if you visit during the week, expect to come across a crowd of schoolchildren whose noise levels might be higher than you'd like.

- **Opening hours** – These vary considerably but at large museums are usually from 9 or 10am to 7 or 8pm. Smaller museums close at lunchtime, e.g. from 2 to 4pm. Most museums close on Mondays (even the Prado) and many open on Sunday mornings only. Many close on public holidays or have reduced opening hours, and most close on 25th December and 1st January. Last access is usually 30 minutes before closing time and visitors are asked to leave 10 or 15 minutes before the museum closes.

● **Entrance fees** – Most museums and galleries charge an entrance fee, ranging from €1.50 to €12. Concessions are available for children (e.g. under 12 at the Guggenheim and under 18 at the Prado), retirees of 65 and over, the unemployed and students. You may have to show proof of your age (e.g. passport) if you ask for a concession ticket. Most museums are free on International Museum Day (18th May), and some museums have other free-entry days, e.g. Sundays at the Prado.

Season tickets are available for many museums, and major cities offer tourist tickets, e.g. the Barcelona Articket, which costs €17 and allows you to visit seven major art museums in the city.

● **Security** – For security reasons, many museums and galleries don't allow visitors inside with belongings other than a handbag. Other types of bag, rucksacks, cameras, umbrellas and coats must be left in a locker or in the cloakroom (*conserje*). Large museums have X-ray machines at the entrance and you may be frisked. Security cameras and (armed) security guards operate in the main galleries.

> **Disabled access**
>
> Most major museums now have disabled access, although you sometimes have to ask to use a lift or stair lift.

● **Displays** – Spain offers some of the best laid-out and most interactive museums in Europe – La Pedrera-Casa Milà in Barcelona and the MUSAC in León are hard to beat in these

City of Arts & Sciences, Valencia

respects – but also some of the least visitor-friendly. Dusty or 'tired' exhibits with minimal explanations or in the regional language only are common. Major museums offer explanations in several languages, including English, although foreign-language explanations are often much shorter than their Spanish equivalent.

- **Cafés & shops** – Eateries and shops in Spanish museums are a relatively new phenomenon and most shops currently offer a limited variety of goods, with the exception of those at children's museums, where acres of paraphernalia such as stuffed and plastic toys and T-shirts is on display. Cafés are often basic and the choice of food limited – the Museo Thyssen-Bornemisza is an exception to this with an elaborate daily *menú*, and the café in the Picasso Museum in Malaga offers gourmet snacks. Prices are similar to those elsewhere in the city, though sometimes higher. Few museums allow you to consume your own food on the premises unless it's in the gardens.

- **Curators** – Spanish museum curators take their job seriously and, although some are happy to share their knowledge with you, most seem to concentrate on stopping you from getting too near exhibits or making sure you go round the museum the right way. Many have an abrupt manner and few smile.

- **Noise** – Spanish museums are mostly quiet places and some curators insist on silence, but the arrival of school parties or tourist groups often puts paid to your rapt

Museum, Monasterio de El Escorial

concentration. Since these groups usually visit at lightning speed, it's best to wait for them to move on before continuing your visit.

SPANISH ARTISTS

Although Spain doesn't have the same prolific tradition in the arts as some other European countries, for example France and Italy, there are nonetheless many key Spanish painters who have had a major influence on the world of art,

PAINTERS

16th and 17th Centuries

El Greco

Domenikos Theotocopuli (1541-1641) was born in Crete, but painted most of his works in Toledo where he gained the nickname, 'El Greco' (The Greek). Influenced by the Byzantine and Venetian schools, El Greco's paintings are characterised by their unusual colours – acid green and blood red dominate – and elongated, mystical figures. 'El entierro del Conde de Orgaz', exhibited in the Santo Tomé church in Toledo, is widely considered to be his masterpiece.

Velázquez

Diego Silva de Velázquez (1599-1660), perhaps Spain's greatest artist, is known as 'the painter of painters' because of his lasting influence on later generations. He was one of the first court painters and under the patronage of Felipe IV, he painted many of his greatest works. He's known for his use of earthy colours, religious topics and portraits. Among his many masterpieces are 'Las Meninas', 'Las Hilanderas' and 'La Rendición en Breda', all on display in the Prado Museum, Madrid.

> 'Las Meninas' by Velázquez was recently restored to its former glory and is now the sole exhibit in one of the rooms in the Velázquez collection in the Prado Museum.

Murillo

Bartolomé Murillo (1617-1682) is one of Spain's most popular artists, known for his use of light and colour and his baroque style. Among his most famous works are 'Niños comiendo melón y uvas' in the Alte Pinakothek, Munich and 'La conversión de San Pablo' in the Prado Museum.

18th and 19th Centuries

Goya

Francisco de Goya (1746-1828) is, along with Velázquez, one of the greatest Spanish masters. He was a prolific artist who was a favourite court painter of Charles IV; his portrait of the royal family entitled

'La familia de Carlos IV' and the 'Majas' – two paintings, one with the Maja dressed and the other nude – are particularly famous. Goya later became deaf as the result of an illness and this, together with the devastating Napoleonic wars, led to his paintings portraying nightmare and monstrous images. The destructiveness and cruelty of war are reflected in his 'Dos de mayo' and 'Tres de mayo' paintings, and the so-called 'black paintings', which include the dramatic canvas entitled 'Saturno devorando a uno de sus hijos', vividly depict social violence. The Prado Museum has a particularly good selection of Goya's masterpieces.

Sorolla

Widely acclaimed as Spain's first 'international' painter when he began exhibiting, Joaquín Sorolla's (1863-1923) works are considered to be essentially Mediterranean. Sorolla developed a unique use of light in his painting, a technique known as 'luminism', which combined with bright pastel colours, form the Sorolla hallmark. His paintings typically represent landscapes in the Levante region of Spain and portraits of fishermen and peasants. Among the most famous are 'Llegada del barco a la playa' and 'Niños en la playa'. His former home in Madrid is now a museum and houses a large collection of his work.

20th Century

Dalí

Surrealism in Spanish painting reached its height in the works of Salvador Dalí (1904-1989) who combined psychoanalysis, dreams and suppressed desire in the majority of his paintings. Melting clocks, lions, ants, elephants (below) and the omnipresent Gala (Dalí's wife) appear in many of his works, among the most famous of which are 'La persistencia de la memoria and 'El Gran Masturbador', exhibited in the Reina Sofía Museum in Madrid (which has the world's best collection of Dali's work).

Gris

The Cubism movement profoundly influenced Juan Gris (1887-1927) who became one of its main Spanish exponents. His paintings, almost all still life, combine everyday objects – newspapers, wine bottles and guitars are recurrent – in visual fragmentation. Among his best-known works are 'Retrato de Josette' and 'Guitarras', on display in the Reina Sofía Museum.

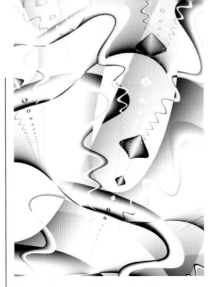

Miró

Joan Miró (1893-1983) belonged to the surrealism movement and developed this in his paintings, mainly characterised by abstract forms in primary colours (red, blue and black dominate). Miró's recurrent symbols are the sun, stars, man and woman set in space, Miró's only landscape, and his work is easily recognisable. An anthology of Miró's work can be seen in the Miró Foundation in Barcelona.

> Miró designed the logo for Spain's largest saving bank, La Caixa. The characteristic logo is a five-pointed blue star with one small red and one small yellow dot next to it.

Picasso

Pablo Ruiz Picasso (1881-1973) is probably Spain's – and the world's – most famous painter, and is considered one of the greatest of all time. This highly versatile artist – Picasso was also a sculptor and ceramist – was influenced by Cubism, surrealism, African art and early Iberian sculpture. Recurrent Picassian images are women and bulls based around the themes of passion and destruction. Picasso's greatest work (at least for the Spanish) is 'Guernica' (housed in the Reina Sofía Museum in Madrid), a huge canvas in black and white depicting the horrors of war and inspired by the atrocities suffered by the inhabitants of the Basque town of Guernica after it was razed to the ground by German bombs at the start of the Spanish Civil War.

Barcelona and Malaga both have comprehensive Picasso museums.

Contemporary Painters

Spain has a thriving artist population and the annual ARCO modern art fair held in Madrid attracts some of the world's best modern art. Among Spain's most famous contemporary painters are Miquel Barceló (born in 1957), famous for his design of Cobi (the Barcelona 1992 Olympics mascot) and his recent ceramic mural in Palma de Mallorca's cathedral; Luis Gordillo (born in 1934), recent winner of the Velázquez Prize for Art and considered by many to be Spain's greatest living artist, and Antoni Tàpies (born in 1923), whose use of collage in his paintings has brought him worldwide acclaim.

SPANISH WRITERS

Spain has produced many great writers and poets, many of whom have achieved worldwide prominence and been recognised internationally, most notably with the Nobel Prize for literature.

Pre 16th Century

'El Poema del Mío Cid'

The earliest surviving Spanish literary text is 'El Poema del Mío Cid', a medieval epic poem describing the adventures of the mercenary knight, El Cid. The text was composed by minstrels in 1140 who recited it, accompanied by music, in court.

Manrique

Jorge Manrique (1440-1479) is Spain's first poet, famous for his poetic ballads (known as *coplas*) with religious themes exalting death and the subsequent encounter with God.

> The anonymous novel, 'Lazarillo de Tormes', published in 1554, is one of Spain's first 'picaresque' novels and tells a tale of a beggar boy who comes across poverty and religious hypocrisy.

16th to 17th Century

This period is known as the 'Golden Age' because of the many playwrights, writers and poets active during this time. Among the best known authors of the Golden Age are:

Cervantes

Miguel de Cervantes (1547-1616) wrote several books, but is most famous for his 'Don Quijote', widely considered to be the world's first novel and certainly one of the most influential. In the novel, Cervantes portrays the parallel worlds of reality and fantasy.

Lope de Vega

Lope de Vega (1562-1635) is one of Spain's most famous and prolific playwrights. In his plays – 'Fuente Ovejuna' and 'El perro del hortelano' are among the best known – honour and love play a major part. Lope de Vega's plays are regularly staged in theatres throughout Spain and several have been made into films.

Calderón de la Barca

Calderón de la Barca (1600-1681) was another playwright and is famous for his philosophical plays (a precursor for modern theatre) whose main characters recite monologues on the meaning of life. Among his best-known works are 'La vida es sueño' and 'El alcalde de Zalamea'.

19th Century Realism

Alas

Leopoldo Alas (1852-1901), better known as Clarín, his pseudonym, was a journalist but is most famous for his novel 'La Regenta', a masterpiece portraying the stifling upper middle class society in a provincial Spanish town and the conflict between what we have and what we would like.

de Castro

Rosalía de Castro (1837-1885) is one of Spain's most famous women writers and her poetry, written in Galician and Spanish, denounced social injustices and poverty in the countryside in 19th century Spain.

Pardo Bazán

Emilia Pardo Bazán (1851-1921) was a keen follower of Emile Zola's naturalism philosophy, and her works were much influenced by the French novelist. 'Los Pazos de Ulloa' and 'Madre naturaleza' are among her most famous novels.

Pérez Galdós

Benito Pérez Galdós (1843-1920) is the Spanish answer to Balzac and Dickens, and the greatest exponent of realism in Spanish literature. A prolific writer of novels, his best-known works include 'Doña Perfecta' and 'Miau', as well as the historical 'Episodios nacionales', a series of 46 novels depicting events in contemporary Spanish history such as the Battle of Trafalgar.

Generation of 1898

This literary movement brought together writers who were alarmed at Spain's ever-increasing social conflict (which culminated in the Civil War) and the end to Spain's world power. Its main proponents were:

Baroja

The philosopher and novelist Pío Baroja (1872-1956) wrote more than 60 novels, many of which tried to explain Spain's history, including 'El árbol de la ciencia'.

Machado

The poet Antonio Machado (1875-1939) had a particularly pessimistic view of Spain and many of his poems portray a divided and violent society. His most famous collection is 'Campos de Castilla'

> Among Machado's most famous lines are:
> "Caminante, son tus huellas el camino, y nada más. Caminante, no hay camino, se hace camino al andar."
> (Traveller, it's your footprints that make the road, and nothing else. Traveller, there's no road, you make the road as you walk along it.)

Unamuno

Miguel de Unamuno (1864-1936) was one of Spain's great philosophers; his most famous works include 'San Manuel Bueno, mártir', the story of a doubting priest trying to convince his congregation of the existence of God, and 'Niebla'.

Generation of 1927

Profoundly influenced by surrealism, this literary movement was mainly formed by poets such as Rafael Alberti, Vicente Aleixandre (Nobel Prize for Literature winner in 1977), Luis Cernuda, Federico García Lorca, Jorge Guillén and Pedro Salinas. Their poetry explores dreams, the subconscious and love.

20th Century Writers

Cela

Camilo José Cela (1916-2002), winner of the Nobel Prize for Literature in 1989, is perhaps the most famous of Spain's recent authors. His first novel, 'La familia de Pascual Duarte', portrays the violence in Spanish society and his later novel, 'La Colmena', depicts the tedium and poverty of post-Civil War Spain.

Delibes

Miguel Delibes (born 1920) is a prolific novel writer whose best-known works include 'El Camino', a portrait of Spanish rural society, 'Cinco horas con Mario', depicting the stifling atmosphere of Franco's dictatorship and 'El hereje' written in 1998.

Contemporary Writers

Although the Spanish aren't known as avid readers – in 2005, only 40 per cent of the population read more than once a week – book fairs are common throughout the country and over 77,000 books were published in 2006. Among the most popular contemporary authors are Javier Marías, Rosa Montero, Antonio Muñoz Molina, Arturo Pérez Reverte and Manuel Rivas, most of whom are also journalists.

> The most popular books in Spain in 2006 were 'The Da Vinci Code' (Dan Brown), 'Don Quijote' and 'The Shadow of the Wind' (Carlos Ruiz Zafón).

9.
RETAIL THERAPY

Shopping in Spain is generally a pleasurable experience as small, family-run shops still constitute the bulk of Spanish retailers. However, shopping 'etiquette' may differ considerably from what you're used to and this chapter provides information on those aspects of shopping that are uniquely Spanish or that you may find surprising.

In small shops it's common to greet the staff and assembled shoppers when you enter and say goodbye when you leave. Many shoppers also exchange pleasantries or gossip and discussions (sometimes heated) often break out among them. This is an essential part of traditional shopping in Spain, where shops are one of the main local meeting places.

CUSTOMER SERVICE

Business in Spain has traditionally focused on products and the production process rather than the people who buy them. This concept is changing and customers are becoming increasingly important.

Customer service (*atención al cliente*) is now given priority in many companies (but by no means all) and large businesses have customer relations departments. In some shops, however, the customer is still way down the owner's list of priorities. When shopping, expect to come across a wide range of service – from surly indifference to couldn't do-more-for-you attentiveness.

Large stores tend to have excellent specialist staff who are trained to go out of their way to help the customer, but in some small shops it can be difficult to get a 'thank you' out of the assistant. If you receive poor service, take your custom elsewhere, as complaining will rarely get you anywhere.

OPENING HOURS

Spanish shops have some of the world's most idiosyncratic opening hours and few shops in the same town open and close at the same time. Shopping hours are generally Mondays to Fridays from 10am to 2pm and from 5 to 8pm, but some shops open at 9.30 or 9.45am, at 4.30 or 5.30pm, some close at 1.30pm and at 9pm, some open on Saturday mornings but not in the afternoon... Fishmongers open mornings only and many are closed on Mondays.

In some towns, shops close one afternoon a week or on Mondays.

On market days, shops tend to stay open all day and don't close for lunch. Some shops close for annual holidays, during local fiestas or for family business.

Supermarkets, hypermarkets and department stores have longer opening hours, e.g. 9.30am to 8.30pm, and don't generally shut at lunchtime. Stores in shopping centres open from 10am to 9pm or 10pm.

Sundays & Public Holidays

Trading on Sundays and public holidays is strictly regulated and in most regions shops open on eight Sundays or public holidays a year only (usually during December and in August). In tourist areas, shops can apply to open on Sundays all year round, but it can be difficult to find a shop open on Sunday afternoons except at petrol stations.

QUEUING

The newcomer to Spain might have the impression that the Spanish don't queue, but in reality there's a complex queuing etiquette that you must master if you want to get served. You won't see many neat lines of waiting customers, but all

> Do as much of your shopping as possible in local shops. This gives you the chance to practise your Spanish and become part of the local community, giving you a sense of belonging.

those in the shop know exactly where their place is in the queue. There are various systems, including the following:

- **ticketing** – Many shops (and counters in supermarkets and hypermarkets) have machines which dispense a numbered ticket and you must wait until your number is displayed over the counter. Sometimes it isn't obvious that you need to take a ticket; if in doubt, you should ask: '*Hay que coger número?*' ('Do I need to take a number?'). If you miss your number, don't expect fellow shoppers to 'allow' you be served before them – miss your number, miss your turn – but simply take another ticket and wait again.

- **enquiring** – When you enter a shop with no ticket system, common practice is to ask who is the last person in the queue: '*Quién es el último?*' (*la última* if it's an all-female queue). The last person says '*Soy yo*' so you know you're after that person.

- **single file** – Single file queuing is common in many banks and government offices, where the first person in the queue goes to the first available desk.

But, although **you** might master the art of queuing, some Spaniards have never managed it. There's always someone who barges in and shouts their order over the heads of everyone else, or who claims to be before you in the queue in spite of the fact that you both know they came in afterwards. It may be worth protesting politely, but it's best to take it in your stride – or make a mental note of how they do it.

SALES

Sales (*rebajas*) are held twice-yearly from 7th January to 28th February and 1st July to 31st August and bargains (*gangas*) can be found everywhere. Spanish shops tend to reduce the prices of current goods rather than bring in 'sales' stock and prices are slashed by up to 60 per cent. In many shops, everything is offered at a discount and sales are an excellent opportunity to buy quality goods at low prices – clothes and shoes are especially good buys.

> Although many goods have marked prices (precio de venta al público/ PVP), these aren't necessarily fixed and in small shops and furniture stores you may get a discount, particularly if you're buying an expensive item or in bulk. But discounts are only offered to those who ask.

The Spanish are keen sales shoppers – though not to the extent of camping overnight outside to make sure they're first in – and shopping centres and department stores are always extremely busy at the start of a sale.

TYPES OF SHOP

With the appearance of shopping centres housing dozens of chain stores open all day throughout the country, the face of Spanish shopping has changed dramatically over the last decade. In most Spanish towns, small, traditional shops are struggling to compete and some forced to close. Many still survive, however, and specialist shops offer an excellent choice of produce and staff with expert knowledge. Among the more unusual Spanish shops are:

- *droguería* – sells toiletries, cosmetics and products for household cleaning, painting, DIY and gardening, but no medicines as you might expect from the name.

- *estanco* – a unique institution in Spain, which therefore doesn't have an accurate English translation. They aren't merely tobacconists' because as well as being the only licensed vendors of tobacco and cigarettes, *estancos* sell stamps, sweets, lottery tickets, postcards, stationery, spirits, tax forms and official forms (e.g. for contracts).

- *ferretería* – not just ironmongers' but treasure troves of household and DIY items where you can buy nails and screws (by weight) and small domestic appliances, have keys cut and get expert advice on how to fix something.

- *kiosko* – another Spanish institution and an omnipresent part of urban street decor. *Kioskos* may be elegant wrought-iron pavilions or decrepit plastic huts, but all sell articles essential for Spanish street life such as chewing gum, sunflower seeds, cold drinks, plastic toys, sweets and ice-creams. Many also sell newspapers and magazines.

- *mercería* – a haberdashery, where you can buy individual buttons, ribbons and braiding by the metre and tights and socks for women and children. Some also sell lingerie.

> Street markets are favourite hunting grounds for petty thieves, who take advantage of the crowds to snatch handbags and wallets. Keep a close eye on your belongings at all times.

Markets

Food Markets

Food markets (*mercado de abastos*) are located in purpose-built buildings in most towns and cities, and are an essential stop on the discerning cook's shopping

round. Markets open Mondays to Saturdays, usually from 8 or 9am to 3pm, when any remaining perishable stock is sold off cheaply. Food markets are popular and the best place for variety and freshness.

Food is usually cheaper than in supermarkets, especially if you buy what's in season and grown locally. Butchers and fishmongers at markets will prepare meat and fish exactly to your specification – a service that isn't offered in many supermarkets.

At markets you shouldn't touch the goods (few stalls are self-service), but you can always ask to taste them – stallholders willingly cut a piece of cheese or ham for customers.

Markets are also an essential meeting point for locals and the place to find out the latest gossip and happenings in a town. Shopping at markets isn't for those in a hurry – queues at stalls often move slowly as each customer has a chat with the stallholder – but an experience to be savoured. If you shop regularly at food markets and get to know stallholders, you can make special orders or ask them to keep items back for you.

Street Markets

Street markets (*mercadillos* or *rastros*) are held at least once weekly in most Spanish towns and cities, starting at around 9am and finishing at 3pm (in southern Spain) or 5 or 6pm (in northern Spain). Stalls generally sell clothes, shoes, fruit and vegetables, flowers, ceramics, CDs and DVDs, art and craft products, jewellery and watches, and leather goods.

They're excellent places for bargains, although goods aren't usually high quality and counterfeit and imitation designer ware, including bags, perfumes, watches and shirts, are commonplace.

Haggling is the norm and you can get substantial discounts, particularly if you're buying several items or go at the end of the day's trading.

FOOD & WINE

The hallmark of Spanish cooking is the use of fresh local produce and, not surprisingly, shopping for food (and preparing it) is a labour of love in Spain, where the quality and range of fresh food is difficult to beat. Many Spanish housewives shop daily, not only because a freshly cooked lunch is expected in many households but also out of enjoyment and the opportunity to socialise.

The Spanish haven't developed a taste for foreign food and wine and are parochial in their tastes (especially in their choice of wine).

This isn't necessarily a problem as Spanish cuisine is one of the most sophisticated and varied in Europe. However, the growing number of foreign residents has led to the introduction of foreign foods in many parts of Spain: yams and plantain bananas are found in many greengrocers'; Marmite and PG Tips sit next to *Cola Cao* and tins of

olives; frankfurters and French pâté share shelf space with *jamón serrano* and *chorizo*; and you can buy spicy, oriental sauces and condiments at most supermarkets.

All non-packaged food is bought by the kilo – shoppers tend to buy by weight, in multiples of 100g (e.g. *doscientos gramos* or *medio kilo*), rather than a number of slices or pieces. Most fresh food must be weighed and priced at the counter, but in some supermarkets cashiers weigh and price fruit and vegetables – find out before you create an irate queue at the check-out.

Meat

The Spanish aren't squeamish about meat and, although you're unlikely to come face to face with a calf's head, expect to see whole chickens, skinned rabbits and pigs' trotters adorning butchers' windows and supermarket meat counters. Meat is cut in a particular way (probably differently from the way you're used to), but a butcher will usually prepare it to your requirements, including boning, filleting or mincing – meat is often minced twice. Chickens are displayed whole (literally) and when you buy one the butcher cuts off the head and claws but leaves the innards unless you

ask for them to be removed. Whole chickens can also be divided into breast fillets, wings and legs.

Pork is **the** Spanish meat and cheap and excellent quality, particularly *ibérico* pork (from free-range pigs who feed exclusively on acorns). Spanish sausages (*salchichas*) are often spicy and/or made of beef, and bacon is thin and fatty, although imported English and Danish cuts are widely available.

Milk

Fresh milk (*leche del día*) is difficult to buy and milk is mostly 'long-life'.

You can buy individual cartons, but most Spaniards buy packs of six one-litre cartons. If you're used to fresh milk, long-life (UHT) milk tastes strange to start with, especially in tea, but you soon get used to it and it has the advantage of not going off in hot weather, though it keeps only for a few days once opened.

Organic Food

Spain's farmers produce acres of organic produce but most is exported to the UK and Germany, and it's frustratingly difficult to buy in Spain itself. Some large supermarkets

> Most shops gift wrap items free of charge: in small shops this is done at the counter, but in larger stores you take the item to a dedicated gift-wrapping counter. There's usually a choice of paper and tag.

Metric/Imperial Conversion

Weight

Imperial	Metric	Metric	Imperial
1 UK pint	0.57 litre	1 litre	1.75 UK pints
1 US pint	0.47 litre	1 litre	2.13 US pints
1 UK gallon	4.54 litre	1 litre	0.22 UK gallon
1 US gallon	3.78 litres	1 litre	0.26 US gallon

Capacity

Imperial	Metric	Metric	Imperial
1 UK pint	0.57 litre	1 litre	1.75 UK pints
1 US pint	0.47 litre	1 litre	2.13 US pints
1 UK gallon	4.54 litres	1 litre	0.22 UK gallon
1 US gallon	3.78 litres	1 litre	0.26 US gallon

Note: An American 'cup' = around 250ml or 0.25 litre.

stock a limited selection of (very expensive) produce and large towns and cities have the odd specialist shop. Organic co-operatives exist in many parts of northern Spain and 'members' can buy organic products.

Free-range eggs and chicken are relatively easy to find, but are around twice the price of 'ordinary' produce.

Wine

Given that Spain has more acres of vineyard than any other country and is the world's third-largest wine producer, it's perhaps not surprising that Spaniards are 'parochial' in their wine tastes – to the point of frowning on other countries' efforts.

It's difficult to find a good choice of wine from elsewhere – even large hypermarkets run to barely a few

shelves of foreign (mostly European) wines – but with 65 official wine-producing areas, there's plenty of Spanish wine to choose from.

Some words for food have other meanings.

- *chorizo* – cured sausage, but also thief or crook. *Choriceo* – thievery.

- *churro* – deep-fried dough sticks or a flop or botched job.
- *coco* – coconut, but also slang for head. *El Coco* is the bogeyman who kidnaps naughty children or those who don't go to sleep.
- *gazpacho* – cold tomato soup, but also mish-mash or hotch-potch, e.g. '*un gazpacho de ideas*'.
- *huevos* – eggs, but also testicles. The expression '*a huevo*' means 'very easy'.
- *leche* – milk or a punch or a crash. '*A toda leche*' means 'as fast as possible', and *leche* is also used as a mild swear word.
- *pollo* – chicken, but '*montar un pollo*' is to make a fuss.
- *pasta* – pasta or a lot of money.

CLOTHES

The quality of clothes in Spain varies from poor to excellent and, as in all countries, you get what you pay for. Cities and large towns

> If you buy an item at a shop that's part of a franchise chain, you must usually return it to the same shop, as other stores in the franchise won't refund or change goods bought elsewhere.

have an excellent choice of fashion outlets to suit all budgets and styles, and most smaller towns have several clothes shops. Spanish style tends to be smart-casual, reflecting the general Spanish obsession with making a good impression, although it's also easy to find more casual clothes. If you're looking for cheap-and-cheerful clothes, try a hypermarket – most stock a wide range of inexpensive clothing for all ages.

Sizes

Spain uses continental sizes for clothes, but, as in many countries, manufacturers interpret these in different ways, therfore it's common

Continental to UK/US Size Comparison

Women's Clothes

Continental	34	36	38	40	42	44	46	48	50	52
UK	8	10	12	14	16	18	20	22	24	26
US	6	8	10	12	14	16	18	20	22	24

Men's Shirts

Continental	36	37	38	39	40	41	42	43	44	46
UK/US	14	14	15	15	16	16	17	17	18	-

Shoes (Women's and Men's)

Continental	35	36	37	37	38	39	40	41	42	42	43	44
UK		2	3	3	4	4	5	6	7	7	8	9	9
US		4	5	5	6	6	7	8	9	9	10	10	11

to find you need one size in one shop but a different one in another – the government has launched a campaign to rectify this situation, due to take effect by 2009. Men's shirts are classed by body size, e.g. small or medium, rather than by collar size. Spanish clothes are generally made for 'smaller' people and if you're very tall and/or large it can be difficult to find clothes that fit.

Shoes

In many shoe shops, you can only try on one pair of shoes at a time or you have to try on one shoe before the shop assistant gives you the other one. Spain now caters for men with larger feet, but few shops stock any women's shoes over size 40 (UK 6-7).

Children's Clothes

You may be surprised at how expensive and elaborate children's clothes are in Spain, where small children (particularly in provincial towns or in middle-class families) are often dressed immaculately to go out. Long shorts with braces for boys and fancy dresses with hair ribbons for girls are common, and both wear patent shoes. Children in the same family are often colour co-ordinated. If you're looking for 'play' clothes, try the larger chain stores such as Zara or hypermarkets.

Alterations

Most clothes shops provide an extensive alteration service – trousers can be taken up or in, sleeves shortened and waists made smaller. Some shops offer this as part of the garment's price and

others make a small charge, e.g. €3 for taking up trousers. If you need an alteration, the shop assistant pins the garment for you. Alterations usually take three days.

COLLECTABLES

The Spanish have a passion for collecting and new collections are launched frequently. Newsagents are full of cardboard packages containing collectables such as doll's house furniture, Disney characters or parts of a model plane or boat.

The first few instalments are usually offered at a discounted price to whet your (or your children's) appetite and the rest at full price. Be aware that most collections run to at least 30 instalments costing around €10 each, making it an expensive hobby. Newspapers regularly offer collections such as encyclopaedias, crime novels, dinner sets and digital cameras – some obtainable by redeeming a coupon, others handed to you in cardboard boxes when you buy your newspaper.

MAIL-ORDER SHOPPING

In general, the Spanish aren't keen on buying goods other than in shops

– some people are suspicious of paying money for a product they haven't seen 'in the flesh' and most people are reluctant to leave delivery of goods in the unreliable hands of the post office.

Internet

Online shopping has been slow to take off in Spain and in consumer surveys Spaniards claim that worries about security are their main reason for not buying via the internet.

However, buying online in Spain is as secure as anywhere else (provided the site is a secure server, with an address beginning https:// rather than http://), and most large retailers offer internet shopping services, the majority using courier companies for delivery rather than the unreliable postal service.

Hypermarkets and some large supermarkets offer online shopping but this has yet to take off, mainly because there's a limited delivery area (e.g. within a 10km radius) and sometimes a minimum amount you must spend, e.g. €80.

Catalogues

Catalogue shopping isn't very popular in Spain. The main problem is the postal service, whose slow or erratic deliveries and insistence that all parcels must be collected from a main post office, mean that it can be weeks before you receive the goods you ordered – just enough time for that 'must-have' garment to have gone out of fashion. Some catalogue companies use couriers, but this adds significantly to the cost of items.

Home Deliveries

Most large supermarkets and all hypermarkets offer home delivery, usually free, but there may be a small charge for delivery of purchases under €50. Furniture and domestic appliance stores usually deliver free to your home, and many companies include the installation of an appliance (e.g. fridge or washing machine) and the disposal of your old one in the price.

RETURNING GOODS

Under Spanish consumer law you have the right to return an item if it isn't suitable or is faulty, but you must return it within the specified period and show proof of purchase (e.g. the receipt). Unsuitable goods must be returned in perfect condition and with their packaging.

The amount of time you have for returning goods depends on the shop and the item, and ranges from five days (e.g. for a computer) to a calendar month (e.g. a pair of trousers). The limit is specified in the shop and on the back of the receipt.

Refunds

Shops aren't obliged to refund your money (although most do) and some provide a credit note (*un vale*) instead (especially during sales).

Refund policy should be displayed

by the tills. If you want a refund on an item bought with a credit or debit card, the refund is made electronically via your card back to your bank account.

Guarantees

Under EU law, all electronic items and appliances have a two-year guarantee and you're entitled to free repair during this period, although you may have to pay a 'call-out' fee for a technician. If an item goes wrong within a month of purchase, you can take it back to the shop where you bought it; any later and you usually have to take the item to a service or repair centre. You're responsible for collecting the item once it has been repaired.

Complaints

To make a complaint, you must complete an official complaint form (*hoja de reclamación*), which all businesses in Spain are required to have by law, and take a copy to your local consumer affairs department (Oficina Municipal de Informaciónal Consumidor/OMIC), which will take action on your behalf against the offending business. If the business is found to be in the wrong, it's penalised. Complaint forms are often powerful consumer tools and sometimes just asking for one means your complaint is resolved by the staff.

Most large towns and all provinces have an OMIC, which can provide information on consumer regulations as well as filing complaints on consumers' behalf. If you have any sort of consumer problem, the OMIC is the best place to start; even if the staff cannot solve the problem themselves, they will usually refer you to the appropriate official body.

The main consumer association in Spain is the Organización de Consumidores y Usuarios (OCU), which has watchdog and educational roles. Ring ☎ 902 300 187 or consult 🖳 www.ocu.org for contact details of your nearest office.

Sagrada Familia, Barcelona

10.
ODDS & ENDS

A country's culture is influenced by various factors and reflected in myriad ways. Among the principal influences are its geography, climate and religion, which are considered here along with miscellaneous cultural manifestations, including crime, the national flag and anthem, government and international relations, pets, time difference, tipping and toilets.

> Ecija is known as the frying pan of Andalusia *(la sartén de Andalucía), with summer temperature*s of around 25°C (95°C).

CLIMATE

One of Spain's main attractions is its climate, particularly on the islands and Mediterranean coast – Tenerife and the Costa Blanca are widely recognised to have 'ideal' climates – where the sun shines for more than 300 days a year and rainy days are few and far between. However, not all of Spain's weather is good news: most of inland Spain has a continental climate with extremes of temperature – Castile is claimed to have 'three months of winter and nine of hell' (*tres meses de invierno y nueve de infierno*) – the latter baking and the former freezing.

The Heat

With the exception of the Canaries and the Atlantic coast, everywhere in Spain is hot in the summer, with temperatures of at least 30°C (86°F) during July, August and often part of September the norm – and parts of Andalusia and Murcia are even hotter. Forest fires often break out in the summer and claim several lives.

Extreme Weather

Rain is often torrential in many parts of Spain and flash flooding is common – often with dangerous consequences: dry river beds can turn into treacherous torrents in minutes, and each year several people are drowned while attempting to cross them. Strong winds frequently blow, particularly on the coasts, and there are occasional tornados. Weather changes **very** quickly in the mountains and hikers are often caught out by high altitude storms, often with fatal consequences.

CRIME

Spain's crime rate is among the lowest in Europe: according to figures released by the Spanish Interior Ministry in 2006, Spain has an incidence of fewer than 50 crimes per 1,000 inhabitants, the lowest in the EU apart from Portugal and Ireland (figures for the UK and Germany are 105 and 80 respectively). This low crime rate is cited by many foreigners as one of their reasons for moving to Spain.

Although the Spanish tend to ignore what they consider 'petty' laws – e.g. parking regulations, noise level restrictions and the requirement to declare your full income to the taxman – most Spaniards show great respect for 'law and order' and great solidarity with the victims of serious crime. Violent crime rates are low and muggings at gun- or knife-point are rare in most towns, although they've increased in recent years in Madrid. It's generally safe to walk anywhere in Spanish cities during the day, but best to avoid narrow streets and bus and train stations after midnight.

FLAG & ANTHEM

Anthem

The Spanish anthem, also known as the 'Royal Spanish March', dates

> Don't underestimate the heat, which is relentless and exhausting, and even dangerous. Do as the Spanish do: stay inside or in the shade during the hottest hours of the day (1 to 5pm), avoid physical exertion and drink plenty of fluids. Older people and children should take particular care.

from the 18th century and is one of the few in the world with no words (although most Spaniards can sing unofficial versions referring unflatteringly to the royal family or Franco). The anthem, whose composer is unknown, was adopted as the national anthem in 1770.

The Second Republic (1931-39) abolished the 'Royal Spanish March' and used an alternative anthem, last played officially in 1939. Some sporting authorities were, however, unaware that the 'Royal Spanish March' had been reinstated; for example, at the Davis Cup final in Melbourne in 2003, the Spanish team stood perplexed to the tune of the Republican anthem!

Flag

The Spanish flag consists of two horizontal red stripes sandwiching a yellow stripe in the middle (the yellow stripe is as wide as the two red stripes together). The flag dates from 1785, when it was chosen as a naval flag because its bright colours allowed the Spanish navy to identify its ships at a distance. Its widespread use came in the 19th century. The Spanish like flags: not just the national flag, which presides over numerous official events and is flown outside most official buildings, but also the EU flag and regional, provincial and local flags – town halls usually fly the Spanish, regional and local flags.

GEOGRAPHY

As well as being the second-largest country in western Europe, Spain is the second highest (after Switzerland) and Madrid the highest capital. Spanish territory occupies most of the Iberian Peninsula and also includes two island groups, the Balearics and Canaries, as well as two North African enclaves, Ceuta and Melilla. These are two of Spain's autonomous regions, which have been held by Spain since the 15th century – not surprisingly, Morocco lays claim to them.

> Spain is referred to as the 'old bull's hide' on account of its shape.
>
> (attributed to Strabo, a first century Roman geographer)

Geographically, Spain is a land of contrasts: great mountain ranges crisscross the landscape, the most notable being the Pyrenees in the north-west (forming a natural barrier between Spain and France); the Cantabrian chain in the north (including the Picos de Europa, whose slopes almost reach the coast); and the Penibetic chain in the south (including the Sierra Nevada with the highest peaks in mainland Spain). The Canary Islands are volcanic mountains jutting out of the Atlantic, and Mount Teide on Tenerife is Spain's highest peak

(3,718m/12,198ft). Elsewhere, you're rarely far from a mountain or high hills except in the centre of mainland Spain, which consists of a

vast plain (the *meseta*) where the landscape undulates but never rises significantly.

Spain has an extensive coastline, and the Atlantic and Mediterranean both wash its shores, which are home to some of Europe's finest sandy beaches. This is a country where you can ski in the Sierra Nevada and swim in the Med on the same day.

In spite of its size, Spain isn't home to many great rivers: the main river is the Ebro, from which the Iberian peninsula gets its name, and others are the Duero, Guadalquivir, Guadiana, Miño and Tagus. Many smaller rivers are usually dry and carry water only during heavy rain, when dusty riverbeds can turn into turbulent floods in minutes. Half of Spain's soil is unproductive or barren and some parts of the south-east are almost desert ('spaghetti' westerns are made in Almería).

In complete contrast, the irrigated regions (*huertas*) of Valencia and the Guadalquivir valley are extremely fertile and Asturias, Galicia and the northern coast of Cantabria are green and lush, with abundant forests and pasturelands.

> Southern Spain is an earthquake zone, although tremors rarely measure more than 5 on the Richter scale or cause more than minor structural damage.

Spain is divided into 17 autonomous regions, most of which have distinct identities, forged in history and proclaimed in local laws, customs and values, although some have been created for political reasons.

GOVERNMENT

Spain has a democratic parliamentary monarchy, which isn't yet half a century old.

The Constitution

Following the death of General Franco in 1975, the Spanish constitution of 6th December 1978 (arguably the most liberal in western Europe) formalised a radical transformation from dictatorship to democracy. The constitution returned power to the regions, which were given their own governments, regional assemblies and supreme legal authorities, while central government retained exclusive responsibility for foreign affairs, external trade, defence, justice, law (criminal, commercial and labour), merchant shipping and civil aviation.

The Constitutional Court (*el tribunal constitucional*) was made responsible for ensuring that laws passed by parliament complied with the constitution and international agreements to which Spain is party.

Changing of the Guard, Royal Palace, Madrid

The Judiciary

The judiciary is independent of the government, the highest legal body being the General Council of Judicial Power (*Consejo general del Poder Judicial*), which has 20 independent members and is headed by the president of the Supreme Court (*tribunal supremo*).

The Monarch

The Spanish monarch (currently King Juan Carlos I) is the head of state and his duties include the endorsement of laws and decrees, the calling of elections and referendums and the appointment of ministers. The monarch is also supreme commander of the armed forces.

The Spanish royal family enjoys considerable popular support and the king is highly respected – he earned much of this respect when, as Franco's successor, he relinquished absolute power in favour of democracy and was instrumental in crushing the 1981 coup. The king works hard at maintaining his popularity – a wise move given the monarchy's history of exile – and is seen very much as a 'people's monarch'. Most Spaniards, however, claim to be '*Juancarlistas*' rather than monarchists and it remains to be seen if they take to Juan Carlos' successor (due to be his son, Felipe).

The royal family pays taxes and is one of the least costly to maintain in Europe as well as boasting a practically scandal-free existence. This may be because the Spanish media have a tacit agreement not to report anything negative about the monarchy and several potential scandals have been hushed up. Satirising the monarchy is almost unheard of and the popular *Guiñol* TV series has latex puppets of most politicians, the Pope, top sportspeople, actors, etc. but no members of the royal family.

> 'There is no country in Europe which is so easy to over-run as Spain; there is no country which is more difficult to conquer.'
> Thomas Babington Macaulay (English poet, historian and politician)

Parliament

The national parliament (*las Cortes Generales*) has two chambers, the lower of which is the Congress of Deputies (*Congreso de los Diputados*) and the upper the Senate (*Senado*). The Congress consists of 350 members, representing Spain's 50 provinces and the North African enclaves of Ceuta and Melilla.

Each province is an electoral constituency, the number of deputies it has in Congress depending on its population.

Members of Congress are elected by a system of proportional representation for four years. The Senate has 259 senators, directly elected by a first-past-the-post system. Each province provides four senators (except the Balearic and Canary Islands, where extra members represent the various islands), making a total of 208; the 17 autonomous regions elect one senator each and an additional senator for each million inhabitants, totalling a further 51. The Senate has the power to amend or veto legislation initiated by Congress.

Political Parties

In 1976, when democracy was born, Spain boasted dozens of small political parties, but 30 years later there are fewer than ten national parties and just two dominate the political scene. The main parties in the current (2004-08) legislature are, in order of the number of seats they hold:

- Partido Socialista Obrero Español (PSOE) – the party currently in power, led by José Luis Rodríguez Zapatero, left-wing (164 seats);
- Partido Popular (PP) – the main opposition party, led by Mariano Rajoy, right-wing (148 seats);
- Convergencia i Unió (CiU) – Catalan Nationalist party, generally right-wing and Catholic (10 seats);
- Esquerra Republicana de Cataluyna (ERC) – Catalan Nationalist party, left-wing and with republican aspirations (8 seats);
- Partido Nacionalista Vasco (PNV) – Basque nationalist party, right-wing and Catholic (7 seats);
- Izquierda Unida (IU) – a coalition of numerous mostly left-wing parties including the communist party and the Greens (5 seats);
- Coalición Canaria (CC) – Canary Islands Nationalist party (3 seats).

INTERNATIONAL RELATIONS

The European Union

Spain is a firm supporter of the EU: this doesn't come as a surprise given the **huge** injection of EU funds into the country since it joined in 1986 – funds that are responsible for a large percentage of Spain's infrastructure. Spain is one of the few countries to have ratified the European Constitution (in 2005) by referendum, and most Spaniards are happy members of the EU club.

> The Spanish Congress is 'guarded' by two large bronze lions, made from melted-down cannons captured from the enemy during the Moroccan (or African) War of 1859-60)

The vast majority of Spaniards accepted the introduction of the euro and support the single currency (even though most still 'think' and talk in pesetas), and the EU flag flies outside public buildings next to the Spanish and regional flags. This attitude may change, however, in 2013, when Spain loses a substantial percentage of its EU funds and goes from being a net receiver to a net contributor.

The World

Spain belongs to all the major international organisations: the United Nations (since 1955), NATO (since 1982) and the EU (since 1986) as well as being a permanent observer member of the Organisation of American States (OAS). The loss of a world empire has never been completely accepted by the Spanish, and foreigners sometimes get the

impression that Spain is still trying to scrabble back onto the world stage. In terms of world politics, however, Spain doesn't usually carry much weight and as a result Spanish politicians often seem to be trying to ingratiate themselves with major foreign powers – notably the US.

Under President Aznar, Spain and the US enjoyed excellent relations – in one well publicised photo, Aznar and Bush share a cigar and a table to put their boots on – and Spain's loyalty went as far as supporting the US in the invasion of Iraq, despite opposition from some 90 per cent of the Spanish population. After he won the elections in 2004, the first election promise to be fulfilled by President Zapatero was to withdraw Spanish troops from Iraq. Since then, relations with the US have been at best lukewarm, at worst chilly.

Spaniards have an ambivalent opinion of the US – they admire its entrepreneur spirit and the economic success of its people but tend to see American culture as 'ignorant'.

A large number of Spaniards also dislike what they see as the US's imperialist tendencies – atrocities in Iraq and the Guantánamo prison are frequent media topics. Many Spaniards despise the fact that the US calls itself 'America' – for a Spaniard, America encompasses the entire continent from Alaska to Patagonia.

Relations with Europe are generally good: Spain feels a natural allegiance towards its immediate European neighbours, and foreign policy emphasises the need for European unity and strength. Spain sees itself as part of 'Old Europe' along with France and Germany, and meetings are often held between leaders of the three countries. Relations between Spain and the UK are also generally good and British news items frequently appear in the media.

Historically, Spain has a strong natural allegiance with Central and South America, and there are many bi-lateral agreements between Spain and her ex-colonies. Central and South America were, for centuries, the destination for thousands of emigrating Spaniards seeking their fortune. Several South American countries, notably Argentina, have large Spanish expatriate populations and many Spaniards have relatives across the Atlantic.

Spain is also a prominent mediator in the Middle East crisis: international peace talks were held in Madrid in 1991, and Spain is the main promoter of the 'Alliance of Civilisations' sponsored by the UN and designed to strengthen ties between the West and the East and, in particular, to help find a solution for the Israeli-Palestinian conflict.

PETS

The Spanish aren't a nation of animal lovers – wild animals are there to be hunted and/or eaten – and only in 2006 was a national law against cruelty to animals approved. Animals are involved in many local festivities, usually as an object of ridicule or to give the locals a chance to show off their prowess – bulls often get the short straw, with bull-running an essential part of many festivities, not just in Pamplona.

> Dogs are often owned as a status symbol and pedigrees are preferred. It isn't unusual for apartment-dwellers to own large breeds such as retrievers and huskies – the latter surprisingly popular in hot, southern Spain. Guard dog breeds, e.g. Alsatian and Rottweiler, are popular with home owners.

Nearly two-thirds of families own pets, dogs and small birds being the most popular, and although they're part of the household, few Spaniards 'spoil' their pets as is common in other countries.

A number of animals are mistreated – it's common to come across chained-up dogs and starving donkeys in the countryside, although their owners usually argue that the animal is serving as a guard or carrier and doesn't deserve 'better' treatment. Hundreds of dogs are abandoned every year, particularly after Christmas and before the summer holidays, and as a result dog homes are packed to bursting point throughout the country. Most Spaniards disapprove of this state of affairs but few take any action to improve it – the vast majority of animal charities and homes are run by foreigners.

RELIGION

According to the Spanish Constitution, Spain is a secular country and although the vast majority of Spaniards are Catholics, significantly less than half of these claim to be either 'religious' or practising Catholics. However, centuries of church influence on the running of the country and its

traditions mean that religion still forms an important part of everyday life. Most Spaniards marry in church, baptise their children and take them to first communion, and practically all fiestas and most public holidays are of religious origin. The Virgin Mary (in numerous guises) is revered throughout Spain and her image adorns cars, necklaces and doorways as well as churches and convents.

The Catholic church isn't self-financing and as such receives considerable public funding (around €270m per year, although the government and church recently agreed to phase this out); it controls many private schools and appoints all religion teachers in the state sector; it owns the COPE radio station (which attracts the second-largest radio audience and is highly critical of the current Socialist government); and it incites Spaniards to defy the latest laws on divorce, homosexual equality and the teaching of ethics in schools.

However, the Catholic church's grip on national affairs is negligible and although religious opposition to certain aspects of government policy is vociferous, it has little effect and the Church's influence is on the wane. The vast majority of young Spaniards don't go to church, an increasing number of children no longer choose to study religion at school and the church has major recruitment problems – most priests and nuns in Spain are now recruited from South America.

Other religions receive an increasingly high profile in the media and there are places of worship representing most denominations in large cities and resort areas.

TIME DIFFERENCE

Most of Spain is on Central European Time (CET), which is Greenwich Mean Time (GMT) plus one hour. The exception is the

The international time difference in winter (October to March) between Madrid at noon (1200) and major cities:

MADRID	LONDON	JO'BURG	SYDNEY	AUCKLAND	NEW YORK
12 noon	11am	1pm	10pm	midnight	6am

Canaries, which from October to March are on Western European Time or GMT and from April to September on CET. The Spanish mainland changes to summer time in spring (the end of March), when they put their clocks forward one hour. In autumn, clocks are put back one hour at the end of September for winter time. Time changes are announced in local newspapers and on radio and television.

Times in Spain, for example in timetables, are usually written using the 24-hour clock, when 10am is written as 10h and 10pm as 22h. Midday (*mediodía*) is 1200 and midnight (*medianoche*) is 2400; 7.30am is written as 07.30. Note, however, that *mediodía* can also refer to lunchtime, which can be anytime between 2 and 4pm. The 24-hour clock is never referred to in speech, when 7am is *las siete de la mañana* and 7pm is *siete de la tarde*.

TIPPING

Tipping isn't a common practice among the Spanish. Hotel, restaurant and café bills usually include a 15 per cent service charge (plus 7 per cent VAT/*IVA* or 16 per cent for 5-fork restaurants), usually shown on the bill as *servicio incluido*. When it isn't indicated, most people assume that service is included. However, even when service isn't included the Spanish rarely leave tips (*propinas*), although they may leave a few small coins. The only exception to this rule is in expensive or fashionable establishments where 'tips' may be given to secure a table (or guarantee a table in future). Many foreigners follow international practice and tip as they would in other countries.

> 'The tipping custom originated in England when small sums were dropped into a box marked T.I.P.S. (TO INSURE PROMPT SERVICE).'
>
> Anon

The 'no tipping' practice usually extends to other businesses and services, including taxi drivers, porters, hotel staff, car park attendants, cloakroom staff, shoeshine boys, ushers (cinemas, theatres and bullrings) and toilet attendants, although you can give a small tip if you wish. Even at Christmas the Spanish rarely give tips, although Spanish employers usually give their employees a hamper or a few bottles of wine. If you're unsure whether you should tip someone, ask your Spanish neighbours, friends or colleagues for advice (who will probably all tell you something different!). Large tips are considered ostentatious and in bad taste in Spain (except by the recipient, who will be your friend for life!).

TOILETS

Although Spain has had a poor reputation in the past for its public toilets (*aseos públicos*), Spanish toilets are now among the cleanest in Europe and most are spotless (although toilet paper is often at a premium). However, you'll still find the occasional dirty toilet (usually at petrol stations), possibly without a seat. Men's urinals are often in full view of passers-by.

The Spanish have a number of words for the toilet, including *servicios* (the most commonly used), *baño* (literally bathroom), *aseos*, *WC*, *retretes* and *sanitarios*. To ask where the toilet is you say '*¿Dónde están los servicios por favor?*' or simply '*¿Hay servicios por favor?*'

> 'The last time I was in Spain I got through six Jeffrey Archer novels. I must remember to take enough toilet paper next time.'
>
> Bob Monkhouse (English comedian)

Public toilets are few and far between in Spain, although there are toilets in bars, cafés, restaurants, hotels, department stores, supermarkets, shopping centres, railway stations, museums and places of interest, on beaches and near markets. Bars, hotels, cinemas and department stores must, by law, offer their facilities free of charge to anyone (although it's customary to buy a drink when using the toilet in a bar or café) but you may need to ask for a key to unlock them. Some cafés and restaurants have their toilets at the rear of the building with access from outside (not from the restaurant). Many public toilets have an automatic light switch and you're plunged into darkness every minute or so.

There are modern coin-operated public toilets with soap, hot water, towels and air-conditioning in some cities and resort areas. The latest craze in plush establishments is for taps that come on when you hold your hands under them. Hand driers are the norm (rather than paper towels), but they're often broken or work for only a few seconds at a time.

One of the reasons is that many Spanish toilets are unable to cope with paper, which should be deposited in the basket provided rather than in the toilet bowl.

Toilet paper (papel higiénico), which is usually very thin in Spain, isn't provided in many toilets and it's advisable to carry some with you when travelling.

APPENDICES

APPENDIX A: EMBASSIES

In Spain

Listed below are the contact details for the embassies of the main English-speaking countries in Madrid. A full list of embassies and consulates in Spain is available from the website of the Ministry of Foreign Affairs (💻 www.mae.es – go to '*servicios consulares*' and then choose the country from the '*Sel. País*' list on the right-hand side).

Australia: ☎ 913 536 600, 💻 www.spain.embassy.gov.au. Consulates are also located in Barcelona and Seville.

Canada: ☎ 914 233 250, 💻 www.canada-es.org. Consulates are also located in Barcelona and Malaga.

Ireland: ☎ 914 364 093. Consulates are also located in Alicante, Barcelona, Bilbao, Las Palmas, Majorca, Malaga (Fuengirola), Seville and Tenerife.

New Zealand: ☎ 915 230 226, 💻 www.nzembassy.com/spain. A consulate is also located in Barcelona.

South Africa: ☎ 914 363 780, 💻 www.sudafrica.com.

United Kingdom: ☎ 917 008 200, 💻 www.ukinspain.com. Consulates are also located in Alicante, Barcelona, Bilbao, Ibiza, Las Palmas, Majorca, Malaga and Tenerife.

United States of America: ☎ 915 872 200, 💻 www.embusa.es. Consulates are also located in Barcelona, Las Palmas, Majorca, Malaga (Fuengirola) and Valencia.

Abroad

Listed below are the contact details for Spanish embassies in the main English-speaking countries. A full list is available at 💻 www.mae.es – go to '*servicios consulares*' and then choose the country from the '*Sel. País*' list on the right-hand side.

Australia: 15 Arkana St, Yarralumla, Canberra, ACT 2600 (☎ 02-6273 3555, 🖥 www.mae.es/embajadas/canberra/es/home).

Canada: 74 Stanley Avenue, Ottawa, K1M 1P4 (☎ 613-747 2252, 🖥 www.mae.es/embajadas/ottawa/es/home).

Ireland: 17A Merlyn Park, Ballsbridge, Dublin 4 (☎ 01-269 1640, 🖥 www.mae.es/embajadas/dublin/es/home).

New Zealand: The Spanish embassy in Australia (see above) also serves New Zealand.

South Africa: 337 Brooklyn Road, Menlo Park, Pretoria 0181 (☎ 12-460 0123, 🖥 www.mae.es/embajadas/pretoria/es/home).

United Kingdom: 39 Chesham Place, London SW1X 8SB (☎ 020-235 5555, 🖥 www.mae.es/embajadas/londres/es/home).

United States of America: 2375 Pennsylvania Ave, NW, Washington, DC 20037 (☎ 202-452 0100, 🖥 www.mae.es/embajadas/washington/es/home).

The business hours of embassies vary and they close on their own country's national holidays as well as on Spanish public holidays. Always telephone to confirm opening hours before visiting.

APPENDIX B: FURTHER READING

English-language Newspapers & Magazines

Unless otherwise stated, telephone numbers are in Spain.

Absolute Marbella (☎ 902 301 130, 🖳 www.absolutemagazine.com). Free monthly magazine.

Barcelona Connect (☎ 933 170 474, 🖳 www.barcelonaconnect.com). Free monthly magazine.

Barcelona Metropolitan (☎ 934 514 486, 🖳 www.barcelona-metropolitan.com). Free monthly magazine.

The Broadsheet (☎ 915 237 480, 🖳 www.thebroadsheet.com). Free monthly magazine.

Costa Blanca News (☎ 965 855 286, 🖳 www.costablanca-news.com). Weekly newspaper published on Fridays.

Costa del Sol News (☎ 952 448 730, 🖳 www.costadelsolnews.es). Weekly newspaper published on Fridays.

Euro Weekly (☎ 952 561 245, 🖳 http://euroweeklynews.com). Weekly free newspaper with editions for the Costa Blanca, Costa del Sol, Costa de Almería, the Heart of Andalusia and Majorca.

Essential Marbella (☎ 952 766 344, 🖳 www.essentialmagazine.com). Free monthly magazine.

The Ibiza Sun (🖳 www.theibizasun.net). Free weekly newspaper.

In Madrid (☎ 915 226 780, 🖳 www.in-madrid.com). Free monthly magazine.

Island Connections (☎ 922 750 609, 🖳 www.newscanarias.net). Fortnightly newspaper published in the Canary Islands.

La Chispa (🖳 www.lachispa.net). Free monthly magazine on natural living in Andalusia.

Lanzarote Gazette (☎ 902 250 750, 🖳 www.gazettelive.com). Free monthly magazine covering Lanzarote and Fuerteventura.

Living Spain (☎ UK 01234-710992, 🖳 www.livingspain.co.uk). Bimonthly lifestyle and property magazine.

The Mallorca Daily Bulletin (☎ 971 788 400, 💻 www.majorca dailybulletin.es). Daily newspaper for the Balearics.

Spain Magazine (☎ UK 0131-226 7766, 💻 www.spainmagazine.co.uk). Monthly lifestyle and property magazine.

Spanish Homes Magazine (☎ UK 020-7633 3333, 💻 www.spanish homesmagazine.com). Monthly property magazine.

Sur in English (☎ 952-649 741, 💻 www.surinenglish.com). Free weekly newspaper.

Tenerife News (☎ 922 346 000, 💻 www.tenerifenews.com). Free fortnightly newspaper.

The Paper (☎ 922 735 659, 💻 www.thepaper.net). Free fortnightly magazine covering Tenerife.

West Coast Magazine (☎ 902 310 313, 💻 http://westcoastmagazine.es). Free monthly magazine covering the western Costa del Sol from Marbella to Sotogrande.

Books

The books listed below are just a selection of the hundreds written about Spain. The publication title is followed by the author's name and the publisher (in brackets). Books prefixed with an asterisk are recommended by the author.

Culture

*A Day in the Life of Spain (Collins)

*Death in the Afternoon, Ernest Hemingway (Grafton)

*In the Garlic, V. Collins & T. O'Shea (Santana)

*In Search of the Firedance, James Woodall (Sinclair-Stevenson)

Spanish Cinema, M. Allinson & B. Jordan (Hodder Arnold)

Spanish Vignettes, Norman Berdichevsky (Santana)

The Cambridge Companion to Modern Spanish Culture, David Thatcher (Cambridge University Press)

*The New Spaniards, John Hooper (Penguin)

History

A Divided Kingdom, The Spanish Monarchy from Isabel to Juan Carlos, John Van Der Kiste (Sutton Publishing)

*****Battle for Spain**, Antony Beevor (Weidenfeld & Nicholson)

Contemporary Spain: A Handbook, Christopher Ross (Hodder Arnold)

*****Ghosts of Spain**, Giles Tremlett (Faber & Faber)

*****Rivers of Gold**, Hugh Thomas (Phoenix Press)

The Defeat of the Spanish Armada, Garrett Mattingly (Pimlico)

The Resilience of the Spanish Monarchy 1665-1700, Christopher Storrs (Oxford University Press)

*****The Spanish Civil War**, Hugh Thomas (Penguin)

The Spanish Civil War: A Very Short Introduction, Helen Graham (Oxford University Press)

The Spanish Civil War: Reaction, Revolution and Revenge, Paul Preston (Harper Perennial)

The Spanish Inquisition, Helen Rowlings (Blackwell Publications)

*****The Triumph of Democracy in Spain**, Paul Preston (Routledge)

Language

Collins Easy Learning Spanish Grammar (Collins)

*****Liz Parry's Spanish Phrase Book**, Liz Parry (Santana Books)

Michel Thomas Foundation Course Spanish, Michel Thomas (Hodder Arnold)

*****Palabra por Palabra**, Phil Turk (Hodder Arnold)

Pardon My Spanish! (Harrap)

Rude Spanish: An Alternative Spanish Phrasebook (Harrap)

*****501 Spanish Verbs**, C. & T. Kendris (Barron's Educational Series)

Living & Working in Spain

******The Best Places to Buy a Home in Spain**, Joanna Styles (Survival Books)

**Costa Blanca Lifeline, Joanna Styles (Survival Books)

**Costa del Sol Lifeline, Joanna Styles (Survival Books)

**Earning Money from your Spanish Home, Joanna Styles (Survival Books)

**Living and Working in Spain, David Hampshire (Survival Books)

*Madrid Inside Out, Arthur Howard & Victoria Montero (Frank)

**Making a Living in Spain, Anne Hall (Survival Books)

*You and the Law in Spain, David Searl (Santana)

Tourist Guides

AA Essential Explorer Spain (AA)

*Andalucía: The Rough Guide (Rough Guides)

*Baedeker's Spain (Baedeker)

*Blue Guide to Spain: The Mainland, Ian Robertson (Ernest Benn)

*Cadogan Guides: Spain, Dana Facaros & Michael Pauls (Cadogan)

*Fodor's Exploring Spain (Fodor's Travel Publications)

*Lonely Planet Spain (Lonely Planet)

*Madrid, Michael Jacobs (George Philip)

Madrid: A Traveller's Companion, Hugh Thomas (Constable)

*Michelin Spain Green Guide (Michelin)

*Michelin Red Guide: España, Portugal (Michelin)

*Spain: The Rough Guide, Mark Ellingham & John Fisher (Rough Guides)

*Special Places to Stay in Spain, Alistair Sawday (ASP)

APPENDIX C: USEFUL WEBSITES

The following list contains some of the many websites dedicated to Spain.

Embassies

Australia (🖳 www.spain.embassy.gov.au). Consulates are located in Barcelona and Seville.

Canada (🖳 www.canada-es.org). Consulates are located in Barcelona and Malaga.

New Zealand (🖳 www.nzembassy.com/spain). Consulates are located in Barcelona.

South Africa (🖳 www.sudafrica.com).

United Kingdom (🖳 www.ukinspain.com). Consulates are located in Alicante, Barcelona, Bilbao, Ibiza, Las Palmas, Majorca, Malaga and Tenerife.

United States of America (🖳 www.embusa.es). Consulates are located in Barcelona, Las Palmas, Majorca, Malaga (Fuengirola) and Valencia.

Spanish Websites

About Spain (🖳 www.aboutspain.net). Information about specific regions.

All About Spain (🖳 www.red2000.com). General tourist information.

Andalucia (🖳 www.andalucia.com). Comprehensive information about the region of Andalusia in English.

Barcelona (🖳 www.xbarcelona.com). Information including job opportunities and useful tips for foreigners living in Barcelona.

Expatica (🖳 www.expatica.com). An excellent compendium of general information about living and working in Spain.

Ideal Spain (🖳 www.idealspain.com). Information about many aspects of living in Spain.

Madrid Man (🖳 www.madridman.com). A wealth of useful and continually updated information about living and working in Madrid, including an 'ask the expert' facility.

Spain Expat (🖥 www.spainexpat.com). Information about living in Spain, including an 'ask the legal expert' facility. The site has particularly good links.

Spain for Visitors (🖥 http://spainforvisitors.com). Good general information about visiting Spain.

Spanish Living (🖥 www.spanish-living.com). Useful general and property information.

Spanish Property Insight (🖥 www.spanishpropertyinsight.com). One of the best websites on property with the emphasis on up-to-date, useful and impartial information. The site includes a forum and a free monthly e-newsletter.

This is Spain (🖥 www.thisisspain.info). Useful general information about moving to Spain.

TurEspaña (🖥 www.tourspain.co.uk or 🖥 www.spain.info). Spanish National Tourist Office .

TuSpain (🖥 www.tuspain.com). General information with the emphasis on buying property and residential matters.

UK in Spain (🖥 www.ukinspain.com). The British embassy's official site includes a wealth of useful information about aspects of living and working in Spain. Go to the 'Consular Information' section and click on the 'Living in Spain' section.

APPENDIX D: REGIONS & PROVENCES

Spain has 17 autonomous regions and 50 provinces, shown on the map opposite and listed below.

Galicia
1. A Coruña
2. Lugo
3. Pontevedra
4. Ourense

Asturias
5. Asturias

Castilla y León
6. León
7. Palencia
8. Burgos
9. Zamora
10. Valladolid
11. Soria
12. Salamanca
13. Avila
14. Segovia

Cantabria
15. Cantabria

La Rioja
16. La Rioja

Pais Vasco
17. Vizcaya
18. Guipúzcoa
19. Alava

Navarra
20. Navarra

Aragon
21. Huesca
22. Zaragoza
23. Teruel

Cataluna
24. Lleida
25. Girona
26. Barcelona
27. Tarragona

Extremadura
28. Cáceres
29. Badajoz

Castilla La Mancha
30. Guadalajara
31. Toledo
32. Cuenca
33. Ciudad Real
34. Albacete

Madrid
35. Madrid

Comunidad Valenciana
36. Castellón
37. Valencia
38. Alicante

Andalucia
39. Huelva
40. Sevilla
41. Córdoba
42. Jaén
43. Cádiz
44. Málaga
45. Granada
46. Almeria

Murcia
47. Murcia

Baleares
48. Baleares

Canarias
49. Santa Cruz de Tenerife
50. Las Palmas de Gran Canaria

France

Asturias
5
Cantabria
15
17
18
País Vasco
19
Navarra
20
Galicia
1
2
3
4
6
Castilla y León
7
8
La Rioja
16
21
24
26
25
Cataluña
9
10
14
11
Aragón
22
27
12
13
30
35
Madrid
23
36
31
32
28
Castilla-La Mancha
Comunidad Valenciana
37
Portugal
Extremadura
29
33
34
38
41
42
Andalucía
Murcia
47
39
40
45
46
44
38
43

Baleares
48

Canarias 49 & 50

APPENDIX E: USEFUL WORDS & PHRASES

On the following pages is a list of words and phrases that you may need during your first few days in Spain. They are, of course, no substitute for learning the language, which you should make one of your priorities. All verbs are provided in the polite *usted* form, which is the correct form to use when addressing a stranger. Where applicable, the feminine form of adjectives has been included (in brackets after the masculine form) – use these if you're a woman.

Asking for Help

Do you speak English?	*¿Habla inglés?*
I don't speak Spanish.	*No hablo español.*
Please speak slowly.	*Hable despacio, por favor.*
I don't understand.	*No entiendo.*
I need ...	*Necesito ...*
I want ...	*Quiero ...*

Communications

Telephone & Internet

landline	*teléfono fijo*
mobile phone	*teléfono móvil* (or simply *móvil*)
no answer	*sin contestar*
engaged/busy	*ocupado*
internet	*internet*
email	*correo electrónico*
broadband connection	*banda ancha/ADSL*
internet café/wifi spot	*internet café/punto wifi*

Post

post office	*oficina de correos*
postcard/letter/parcel	*tarjeta postal/carta/paquete*
stamps	*sellos*
How much does it cost to send a letter to Europe/North America/Australia?	*¿Cuánto cuesta mandar una carta a Europa/Norte América/Australia?*

Media

newspaper/magazine	*periódico/revista*
Do you sell English-language media?	*¿Vende prensa en inglés?*

Courtesy

yes	*sí*
no	*no*
excuse me	*perdón* or *discúlpeme*
sorry	*lo siento* or *perdón*
I don't know	*no sé*
I don't mind	*no me importa*
please	*por favor*
thank you	*gracias*
you're welcome	*de nada*

Days & Months

All days and months are written with a small initial letter in Spanish.

Monday	*lunes*
Tuesday	*martes*
Wednesday	*miércoles*
Thursday	*jueves*
Friday	*viernes*
Saturday	*sábado*
Sunday	*domingo*
January	*enero*
February	*febrero*
March	*marzo*
April	*abril*
May	*mayo*
June	*junio*
July	*julio*
August	*agosto*
September	*setiembre*
October	*octubre*
November	*noviembre*
December	*diciembre*

Driving

car insurance	*seguro de coche*
driving licence	*permiso de conducir*
hire/rental car	*coche de alquiler*
How far is it to ...?	*¿Qué distancia hay a ...?*
Can I park here?	*¿Puedo aparcar aquí?*
unleaded petrol (gas)/diesel	*gasolina sin plomo/diésel*
Fill the tank up, please.	*Lleno, por favor.*
I need €20/30/40 of petrol (gas).	*Necesito €20/30/40 de gasolina.*
air/water/oil	*aire/agua/aceite*
car wash	*lavado de coche*
My car has broken down.	*Mi coche está averiado.*
I've run out of petrol (gas).	*Estoy sin gasolina.*
The tyre is flat.	*Tengo un pinchazo.*
I need a tow truck.	*Necesito una grúa.*

Emergency

Emergency!	*¡Emergencia!*
Fire!	*¡Fuego!*
Help!	*¡Socorro!*
Police!	*¡Policía!*
Stop!	*¡Pare!*
Stop thief!	*¡Ladrón!*
Watch out!	*¡Cuidado!*

Finding your Way

Where is ...?	*¿Dónde está ...?*
Where is the nearest ...?	*¿Dónde está el ... más cercano?*
How do I get to ...?	*¿Por dónde voy a ...?*
Can I walk there?	*¿Puedo ir andando?*
How far is ....?	*¿Cómo de lejos está ...?*
A map, please.	*Un mapa/plano, por favor.*
I'm lost.	*Estoy perdido (perdida).*
left/right/straight ahead	*izquierda/derecha/todo recto*
opposite/next to/near	*enfrente/al lado de/cerca*
airport	*aeropuerto*
bus/plane/taxi/train	*autobús/avión/taxi/tren*
bus stop	*parada de autobús*
taxi rank	*parada de taxi*

train/bus station	*estación de tren/autobús*
When does the ... arrive/leave?	*¿A qué hora llega/sale ...?*
one-way/return ticket	*billete de ida/ida y vuelta*
bank/embassy/consulate	*banco/embajada/consulado*

Greetings

Hello.	*Hola.*
Goodbye.	*Adiós.*
Good morning.	*Buenos días.*
Good afternoon.	*Buenas tardes.*
Good night.	*Buenas noches.*

Health & Medical Emergencies

I feel ill/dizzy.	*Me siento mal/ mareado(mareada).*
I need a doctor/ambulance.	*Necesito un médico/una ambulancia.*
doctor/nurse/dentist	*médico/enfermera/dentista*
surgeon/specialist	*cirujano/especialista*
hospital/healthcentre/A&E	*hospital/centro de salud/ urgencias*
chemist/optician	*farmacia/óptica*
prescription	*receta*

Other phrases for medical emergencies are given in **Chapter 3**.

In a Bar or Restaurant

Waiter!	*¡Camarero!*
menu	*carta*
bill	*cuenta*
well done/medium/rare (for meat)	*muy hecho/medio hecho/poco hecho*
vegetarian	*vegetariano*
meat/fish	*carne/pescado*

Numbers

one	*uno*
two	*dos*
three	*tres*
four	*cuatro*
five	*cinco*
six	*seis*
seven	*siete*
eight	*ocho*
nine	*nueve*
ten	*diez*
eleven	*once*
twelve	*doce*
thirteen	*trece*
fourteen	*catorce*
fifteen	*quince*
sixteen	*dieciséis*
seventeen	*diecisiete*
eighteen	*dieciocho*
nineteen	*diecinueve*
twenty	*veinte*
thirty	*treinta*
forty	*cuarenta*
fifty	*cincuenta*
sixty	*sesenta*
seventy	*setenta*
eighty	*ochenta*
ninety	*noventa*
100	*cien*
200	*doscientos*
500	*quinientos*
1,000	*mil*

Paying

How much is it?	*¿Cuánto es?*
The bill, please	*La cuenta, por favor.*
Do you take credit cards?	*¿Aceptan tarjetas de crédito?*

Socialising

Pleased to meet you.	*Encantado(Encantada).*
My name is ...	*Me llamo ...*
This is my husband/wife/	*Este es mi marido/*
son/daughter/colleague	*esposa/hijo/hija/compañero*
How are you?	*¿Cómo está?*
Very well, thank you.	*Muy bien, gracias.*

Shopping

What time do you open/close?	*¿A qúe hora abre/cierra?*
Who's the last person?	*¿Quién es el último?*
I'm just looking (browsing).	*Sólo estoy mirando.*
I'm looking for ...	*Busco ...*
Can I try it on?	*¿Puedo probarlo?*
I need size ...	*Necesito la talla ...*
bigger/smaller/longer/shorter	*más grande/pequeño/largo/*
	corto
A bag, please.	*Una bolsa, por favor.*
How much is this?	*¿Cuánto es?*

INDEX

Survival Books

Survival Books was established in 1987 and by the mid-'90s was the leading publisher of books for people planning to live, work, buy property or retire abroad.

From the outset, our philosophy has been to provide the most comprehensive and up-to-date information available. Our titles routinely contain up to twice as much information as other books and are updated frequently. All our books contain colour photographs and some are printed in two colours or full colour throughout. They also contain original cartoons, illustrations and maps.

Survival Books are written by people with first-hand experience of the countries and the people they describe, and therefore provide invaluable insights that cannot be obtained from official publications or websites, and information that is more reliable and objective than that provided by the majority of unofficial sites.

Survival Books are designed to be easy – and interesting – to read. They contain a comprehensive list of contents and index, and extensive appendices, including useful addresses, further reading, useful websites and glossaries to help you obtain additional information as well as metric conversion tables and other useful reference material.

Our primary goal is to provide you with the essential information necessary for a trouble-free life or property purchase and to save you time, trouble and money.

We believe our books are the best – they are certainly the best-selling. But don't take our word for it – read what reviewers and readers have said about Survival Books at the front of this book.

Buying a Home Series

Buying a home abroad is not only a major financial transaction but also a potentially life-changing experience; it's therefore essential to get it right. Our Buying a Home guides are required reading for anyone planning to purchase property abroad and are packed with vital information to guide you through the property jungle and help you avoid disasters that can turn a dream home into a nightmare.

The purpose of our Buying a Home guides is to enable you to choose the most favourable location and the most appropriate property for your requirements, and to reduce your risk of making an expensive mistake by making informed decisions and calculated judgements rather than uneducated and hopeful guesses. Most importantly, they will help you save money and will repay your investment many times over.

Buying a Home guides are the most comprehensive and up-to-date source of information available about buying property abroad – whether you're seeking a detached house or an apartment, a holiday or a permanent home (or an investment property), these books will prove invaluable.

For a full list of our current titles, visit our website at
www.survivalbooks.net

Living and Working Series

Our Living and Working guides are essential reading for anyone planning to spend a period abroad – whether it's an extended holiday or permanent migration – and are packed with priceless information designed to help you avoid costly mistakes and save both time and money.

Living and Working guides are the most comprehensive and up-to-date source of practical information available about everyday life abroad. They aren't, however, simply a catalogue of dry facts and figures, but are written in a highly readable style – entertaining, practical and occasionally humorous.

Our aim is to provide you with the comprehensive practical information necessary for a trouble-free life. You may have visited a country as a tourist, but living and working there is a different matter altogether; adjusting to a new environment and culture and making a home in any foreign country can be a traumatic and stressful experience. You need to adapt to new customs and traditions, discover the local way of doing things (such as finding a home, paying bills and obtaining insurance) and learn all over again how to overcome the everyday obstacles of life.

All these subjects and many, many more are covered in depth in our Living and Working guides – don't leave home without them.

The Survival Handbooks!

Culture Wise Series

Our *Culture Wise* series of guides is essential reading for anyone who wants to understand how a country really 'works'. Whether you're planning to stay for a few days or a lifetime, these guides will help you quickly find your feet and settle into your new surroundings.

Culture Wise guides:
• Reduce the anxiety factor in adapting to a foreign culture
• Explain how to behave in everyday situations in order to avoid cultural and social gaffes
• Help you get along with your neighbours, make friends and establish lasting business relationships
• Enhance your understanding of a country and its people.

People often underestimate the extent of cultural isolation they can face abroad, particularly in a country with a different language. At first glance, many countries seem an 'easy' option, often with millions of visitors from all corners of the globe and well-established expatriate communities. But, sooner or later, newcomers find that most countries are indeed 'foreign' – and many come unstuck as a result.

Culture Wise guides will enable you to quickly adapt to the local way of life and feel at home, and – just as importantly – avoid the worst effects of culture shock.

The essential guides to Culture, Customs & Business Etiquette

Other Survival Books

Investing in Property Abroad: Essential reading for anyone planning to buy property abroad, containing surveys of over 30 countries.

The Best Places to Buy a Home in France/Spain: Unique guides to where to buy property in France and Spain, containing detailed regional profiles and market reports.

Buying, Selling and Letting Property: The best source of information about buying, selling and letting property in the UK.

Earning Money From Your Home: Income from property in France and Spain, including short- and long-term letting.

Foreigners in France/Spain: Triumphs & Disasters: Real-life experiences of people who have emigrated to France and Spain, recounted in their own words.

Making a Living: Comprehensive guides to self-employment and starting a business in France and Spain.

Renovating & Maintaining Your French Home: The ultimate guide to renovating and maintaining your dream home in France.

Retiring in France/Spain: Everything a prospective retiree needs to know about the two most popular international retirement destinations.

Running Gîtes and B&Bs in France: An essential book for anyone planning to invest in a gîte or bed & breakfast business in France.

Rural Living in France: An invaluable book for anyone seeking the 'good life', containing a wealth of practical information about all aspects of French country life.

Shooting Caterpillars in Spain: The hilarious and compelling story of two innocents abroad in the depths of Andalusia in the late '80s.

Wild Thyme in Ibiza: A fragrant account of how a three-month visit to the enchanted island of Ibiza in the mid-'60s turned into a 20-year sojourn.

For a full list of our current titles, visit our website at
www.survivalbooks.net

📷 Photo Credits

DATE DUE